The Divine Mission
of Jesus Christ

The Divine Mission
of Jesus Christ

Alma P. Burton

Cover artwork by: Del Parson

Granite Publishing and Distribution, L.L.C.
270 South Mountainlands Drive Suite 7
Orem, UT 84058

(801) 229-9023 • (800) 574-5779 • FAX (801) 229-1924

ISBN: 1-57636-041-5
Library of Congress Catalog Card Number: 97-68371
Typeset/Designed by: *SunRise Publishing, Orem, Utah*

To

Clea

FOREWORD

The author and the Publisher are aware that quoting large blocks of material is usually done by reducing the size of the print and blocking the material to show that such material is not the work of the author but is a quotation. However, the materials in this book are printed in the same size of type both for the original work of the author and all the quotations used. Quotations "..." and proper documentation at the end of the quotation will identify the quotation from the original work of the author.

This method is being used to make for an easier flow of the materials to promote an ease in reading, not necessitating a change in the size of the type being used as the reader proceeds from page to page.

ACKNOWLEDGMENTS

"What I the Lord have spoken, I have spoken, and I excuse not myself; and though the heavens and the earth pass away, my word shall not pass away, but shall all be fulfilled, whether by mine own voice or by the voice of my servants, it is the same." (D&C 1:38)

Therefore, the author acknowledges the words of the Lord Jesus Christ and those of His chosen leaders of the Church of Jesus Christ of Latter-day Saints that have been quoted in this book, *The Divine Mission of Jesus Christ.*

Sincere appreciation is expressed to my son, James R. Burton, for his sustained interest and encouragement regarding this work: To his children, Brenda and Jeffrey, for reading the manuscript and for making helpful suggestions on it: to my son, John C. Burton for special assistance; to Melinda Blake Taylor, a granddaughter, and to Caralee Garner Hill, for typing the manuscript.

Key to Abbreviations

Books of the Bible, Book of Mormon and Pearl of Great Price are designated by name, or the usual abbreviations. For other references, these abbreviations are used.

NWAF	A New Witness for the Articles of Faith, Bruce R. McConkie
AF	Articles of Faith, James E. Talmage
CR.	Conference Reports
DNCS	Deseret News Church Section
DPJS	Discourses of the Prophet Joseph Smith, Compiled by Alma P. Burton
D&C	Doctrine and Covenants
DS	Doctrines of Salvation, Joseph Fielding Smith Compiled by Bruce R. McConkie
GG	The Government of God, John Taylor
GT	Gospel Truth Vol 1 and 2, published 1957, George Q. Cannon
HC	History of the Church, Joseph Smith
IE	Improvement Era
IV	Inspired Version of the Bible
JTC	Jesus the Christ, James E. Talmage
JD	Journal of Discourses
MA	Mediation and Atonement, John Taylor
MD	Mormon Doctrine, Bruce R. McConkie
MS	Millennial Star
SME	Sermons and Missionary Experiences of Melvin J. Ballard, Bryant S. Hinckley
SMH	Stories from Mormon History, Alma P. and Clea M. Burton
TNT	Toward the New Jerusalem, Alma P. Burton
WP	The Way to Perfection, Joseph Fielding Smith

TABLE OF CONTENTS

Chapter One
Jesus Christ—God Of This World

The Prophet Joseph Smith and Oliver Cowdery testified that our Lord and Savior Jesus Christ appeared to them, ministered to them, and gave them instructions. Their testimony has gone forth to all the world for more than one hundred years. "The Lord Jesus Christ," whom they saw, "Is heir of this Kingdom and holds the keys over all this world." At another time the Prophet Joseph Smith said: "I want to set it forth in a plain and simple manner, that to us there is but one God—that is pertaining to us, and he is in all and through all ... I say there are Gods many and Lords many, but to us only one and we are in subjection to that one." (DPJS, 36)

Abraham revealed how the Savior was appointed to his divine mission as the God of this Earth.

"Now the Lord had shown unto me, Abraham, the intelligences that were organized before the world was; and among all these there were many of the noble and great ones;

"And God saw these souls that they were good, and he stood in the midst of them, and he said: These I will make my rulers, for he stood among those that were spirits, and he saw that they were good; and he said unto me: Abraham, thou art one of them; thou wast chosen before thou wast born.

"And there stood one among them that was like unto God, and he said unto those who were with him: We will go down, for there is space there, and we will take of these materials, and we will make an earth whereon these may dwell;

"And we will prove them herewith, to see if they will do all things whatsoever the Lord their God shall command them;

"And they who keep their first estate shall be added upon; and they who keep not their first estate shall not have glory in the same kingdom with those who keep their first estate; and they who keep their second estate shall have glory added upon their heads for ever and ever.

"And the Lord said: Whom shall I send? And one answered like unto the Son of Man: Here am I, send me. And another answered and said: Here am I, send me. And the Lord said: I will send the first.

"And the second was angry, and kept not his first estate; and, at that day, many followed after him." (Abraham 3:22-28)

The Prophet Joseph Smith explained that: "The contention in heaven was—Jesus said there would be certain souls that would not be saved; and the devil said he would save them all, and laid his plans before the grand council, who gave their vote in favor of Jesus Christ. So the devil rose up in rebellion against God, and was cast down with all who put up their heads for him. (DPJS, 130)

"At the first organization in Heaven we were all present, and saw the Savior chosen and appointed, and the plan of salvation made, and we sanctioned it." (DPJS, 77) And then the Prophet presented his knowledge of the mission of Jehovah, "The great Jehovah contemplated the whole of the events connected with the earth, pertaining to the plan of salvation before it rolled into existence, or ever "the morning stars sang together" for joy; the past, the present, and the future were and are, with him, one eternal "now." He ordered all things according to the council of his own will; he knows the situation of both the living and the dead, and has made ample provision for their redemption, according to their several circumstances, and the laws of the kingdom of God, whether in this world, or in the world to come." (DPJS, 77)

Elder James E. Talmage has written; "We claim scriptural authority for the assertion that Jesus Christ was and is God the Creator, the God who revealed Himself to Adam, Enoch, and all the antediluvial patriarchs and prophets down to Noah; the God of Abraham, Isaac and Jacob; the God of Israel as a united people, and the God of Ephraim and Judah after the disruption of the Hebrew nation; the God who made Himself known to the prophets from Moses to Malachi; the God of the Old Testament record; and the God of the Nephites. We affirm that Jesus Christ was and is Jehovah, the Eternal One." (*Jesus the Christ*, pg. 32)

Now let us consider some of the events of the Savior's life on earth. The Angel Gabriel came to Mary to inform her that she had found favor with the Lord and that her son was to be called "Son of the Highest."

"...in the sixth month the angel Gabriel was sent from God unto a city of Galilee, named Nazareth,

"To a virgin, espoused to a man whose name was Joseph, of the house of David; and the virgin's name was Mary.

"And the angel came in unto her and said, Hail, thou virgin, who art highly favored of the Lord. The Lord is with thee, for thou art chosen and blessed among women.

"And when she saw the angel, she was troubled at his saying, and pondered in her mind what manner of salutation this should be.

"And the angel said unto her, Fear not Mary: for thou hast found favor with God.

"And behold, thou shalt conceive, and bring forth a son, and shall call his name Jesus.

He shall be great, and shall be called the Son of the Highest; and the Lord God shall give unto him the throne of his father David;

"And he shall reign over the house of Jacob forever; and of his kingdom there shall be no end.

"Then said Mary unto the angel; How shall this be?

"And the angel answered and said unto her, of the

Holy Ghost, and the power of the Highest. Therefore also, that holy child that shall be born of thee shall be called the Son of God." (IV, Luke 1:26-35)

Elder Melvin J. Ballard commented on the words of Luke regarding Mary's becoming the virgin mother of the Son of God:

"One of the great questions that I have referred to that the world is concerned about, and is in confusion over, is as to whether or not his was a virgin birth, a birth wherein divine power interceded. Joseph Smith made it perfectly clear that Jesus Christ told the absolute truth, as did those who testify concerning him, the Apostles of the Lord Jesus Christ, wherein he is declared to be the very Son of God. And if God the Eternal Father is not the real Father of Jesus Christ, then we are in confusion; then is he not in reality the Son of God. But we declare that he is the Only Begotten of the Father in the flesh.

"Mary told the story most beautifully when she said that an angel of the Lord came to her and told her that she had found favor in the sight of God, and had come to be worthy of the fulfillment of the promises heretofore made, to become the virgin mother of the Redeemer of the world. She afterward, referring to the event, said: "God hath done wonderful things to me." "And the Holy Ghost came upon her," in the story, "and she came into the presence of the highest." No man or woman can live in mortality and survive the presence of the Highest except by the sustaining power of the Holy Ghost. So it came upon her to prepare her for admittance into the divine presence and the power of the Highest, who is the Father, was present, and overshadowed her, and the holy Child that was born of her was called the Son of God.

"Men who deny this, or who think that it degrades our Father, have no true conception of the sacredness of the most marvelous power with which God has endowed mortal men—the power of creation. Even though that power may be abused and may become a harp of mere pleasure to the wicked, nevertheless, it is the most sacred and holy and divine function with which God has endowed men. Made holy, it is retained by the Father of us all, and in his exercise of that great and marvelous creative power and function, he did not debase himself, degrade himself, nor debauch his daughter. Thus Christ became the literal Son of a divine Father, and no one else was worthy to be his father. (Bryant S. Hinckley, *Sermons and Missionary Services of Melvin J. Ballard,* pp.166, 167)

We are indebted to Luke for one of the accounts of the Savior's Birth:

"And it came to pass in those days, that there went out a decree from Caesar Augustus, that all his empire should be taxed.

"This same taxing was when Cyrenius was governor of Syria.

"And all went to be taxed, everyone in his own city.

"And Joseph also went up from Galilee, out of the city of Nazareth, into Judea, unto the city of David, which is called Bethlehem: (because he was of the house and lineage of David,)

"To be taxed, with Mary his espoused wife, she being great with child.

"And so it was, that, while they were there, the days were accomplished that she should be delivered.

"And she brought forth her firstborn son, and

wrapped him in swaddling clothes, and laid him in a manger, because there was none to give room for them in the inns.

"And there were in the same country, shepherds abiding in the field, keeping watch over their flocks by night.

"And lo, an angel of the Lord appeared unto them, and the glory of the Lord shone round about them; and they were sore afraid.

"But the angel said unto them, Fear not, for behold, I bring you good tidings of great joy, which shall be to all people.

"For unto you is born this day, in the city of David, a Savior, who is Christ the Lord.

"And this is the way you shall find the babe, he is wrapped in swaddling clothes, and is lying in a manger.

"And suddenly there was with the angel a multitude of the heavenly host praising God, and saying,

"Glory to God in the highest; and on earth, peace; goodwill to men." (IV, Luke 2:1-14)

Matthew recorded the baptism of Jesus by John in the river Jordan and John heard the voice of the Father:

"This is my beloved Son, in whom I am well pleased. Hear ye him."

"Thus came John, preaching and baptizing in the river of Jordan; bearing record, that he who was coming after him had power to baptize with the Holy Ghost and fire.

"And then cometh Jesus from Galilee to Jordan, unto John, to be baptized of him;

"But John refused him, saying, I have need to be baptized of thee, and why comest thou to me?

"And Jesus, answering, said unto him, Suffer me to be baptized of thee, for thus it becometh us to fulfill all righteousness. Then he suffered him.

"And John went down into the water and baptized him.

"And Jesus when he was baptized, went up straightway out of the water; and John saw, and lo, the heavens were opened unto him, and he saw the Spirit of God descending like a dove and lighting upon Jesus.

"And lo, he heard a voice from heaven, saying, This is my beloved Son, in whom I am well pleased. Hear ye him." (IV, Matthew 3:40-46)

The prophet Joseph Smith revealed that the Holy Ghost came in the sign of the dove, He said:

"Whoever led the Son of God into the waters of baptism, and had the privilege of beholding the Holy Ghost descend in the form of a dove, or rather in the sign of the dove, in witness of that administration? The sign of the dove was instituted before the creation of the world, a witness for the Holy Ghost, and the devil cannot come in the sign of a dove. The Holy Ghost is a personage, and is in the form of a personage. It does not confine itself to the form of the dove, but in sign of the dove. The Holy Ghost cannot be transformed into a dove; but the sign of a dove was given to John to signify the truth of the deed, as the dove is an emblem or token of truth and innocence." (DPJS, 98)

John the Beloved recorded his testimony of the Only Begotten Son of God. His account is from the Inspired Version by the Prophet Joseph Smith.

"In the beginning was the gospel preached through the Son. And the gospel was the word, and the word was with the Son, and the Son was with God, and the Son was of God.

"The same was in the beginning with God.

"All things were made by him; and without him was not anything made which was made.

"In him was the gospel, and the gospel was the life, and the life was the light of men;

"And the light shineth in the world, and the world perceiveth it not....

"He came unto his own, and his own received him not.

"But as many as received him, to them gave he power to become the sons of God; only to them who believe on his name.

"He was born, not of blood, nor of the will of the flesh, nor of the will of man, but of God.

"And the same word was made flesh, and dwelt among us, and we beheld his glory, the glory as of the Only Begotten of the Father, full of grace and truth.

"John bear witness of him, and cried, saying, This is he of whom I spake; He who cometh after me, is pre-ferred before me; for he was before me.

"For in the beginning was the Word, even the Son, who is made flesh, and sent unto us by the will of the

Father. And as many as believe on his name shall receive of his fullness. And of his fullness have all we received, even immortality and eternal life, through his grace.

"For the law was given through Moses, but life and truth came through Jesus Christ....

"And no man hath seen God at any time, except he hath borne record of the Son; for except it is through him no man can be saved." (IV, John 1:1-5, 11-17,19)

Simeon and Anna witnessed that the youth they saw in the temple was the Lord's Christ.

"And behold, there was a man at Jerusalem, whose name was Simeon; and the same man was just and devout, waiting for the consolation of Israel; and the Holy Ghost was upon him.

"And it was revealed unto him by the Holy Ghost, that he should not see death before he had seen the Lord's Christ.

"And he came by the Spirit into the temple; and when the parents brought in the child, even Jesus, to do for him after the custom of the law,

"Then took he him up in his arms, and blessed God, and said.

"Lord, now lettest thy servant depart in peace, according to thy word;

"For mine eyes have seen thy salvation....

"And there was one Anna, a prophetess, the daughter of Phanuel, of the tribe of Asher. She was of great age, and had lived with a husband only seven years, whom she married in her youth.

"And she lived a widow about fourscore and four years, who departed not from the temple, but served God with fasting and prayers, night and day.

"And she, coming in that instant, gave thanks likewise unto the Lord, and spake of him, to all those who looked for redemption in Jerusalem.

"And when they had performed all things according to the law of the Lord, they returned into Galilee to their own city, Nazareth.

"And the child grew, and waxed strong in spirit, being filled with wisdom, and the grace of God was upon him.

"And Jesus increased in wisdom and stature, and in favor with God and man." (IV, Luke 2:25-30, 36-40, 52)

Elder James E. Talmage explained about Jewish boys going to the temple at age twelve.

"When Jesus had attained the age of twelve years He was taken by His mother and Joseph to the feast as the law required; whether the Boy had ever before been present on such an occasion we are not told. At twelve years of age a Jewish boy was recognized as a member of his home community.... It was the common and very natural desire of parents to have their sons attend the feast of the Passover and be present at the temple ceremonies." (*Jesus the Christ*, p.113)

The Inspired Version of the Bible translated by the prophet Joseph Smith gives us added information about Jesus' youth.

"Jesus grew up with his brethren, and waxed strong, and waited upon the Lord for the time of his ministry to come. And he served under his father, and he spake not as other men, neither could he be taught; for he needed not that any man should teach him. And after many years, the hour of his ministry drew nigh." (IV, Matthew 3:24-26)

The Savior had enjoyed great success in his ministry in Judea, and then—

"...he came to Nazareth, where he had been brought up; and as his custom was he went into the synagogue on the Sabbath day, and stood up to read.

"And there was delivered unto him the book of the prophet Esaias. And when he had opened the book, he found the place where it was written.

"The Spirit of the Lord is upon me, because he hath anointed me to preach the gospel to the poor, he hath sent me to heal the broken-hearted, to preach deliverance to the captives, and the recovering of sight to the blind; to set at liberty them that are bruised;

"To preach the acceptable year of the Lord.

"And he closed the book, and he gave it again to the minister, and he sat down.

"And the eyes of all those who were in the synagogue, were fastened on him. And he began to say unto them, This day is this scripture fulfilled in your ears.

"And all bare him witness, and wondered at the gracious words which proceeded out of his mouth. And they said, Is not this Joseph's son?

"And he said unto them, Ye will surely say unto me this proverb, Physician, heal thyself. Whatsoever we have heard was done in Capernaum, do also here in thy country.

"And he said, Verily I say unto you, No prophet is accepted in his own country.

"But I tell you the truth, many widows were in Israel in the days of Elias, when the heaven was shut up three years and six months, and great famine was throughout all the land;

"But unto none of them was Elias sent, save unto Sarepta, of Sidon, unto a woman who was a widow.

"And many lepers were in Israel, in the time of Eliseus the prophet; and none of them were cleansed, save Naaman the Syrian.

"And all they in the synagogue, when they heard these things, were filled with wrath,

"And rose up, and thrust him out of the city, and led him unto the brow of the hill whereon their city was built, that they might cast him down headlong.

"But he, passing through the midst of them, went his way." (IV, Luke 4:16-30)

We learn from Abinadi in the Book of Mosiah, in the Book of Mormon, that Jesus Christ is both the Father and the Son.

"And now Abinadi said unto them: I would that ye should understand that God himself shall come down among the children of men, and shall redeem his people.

"And because he dwelleth in flesh he shall be called the Son of God, and having subjected the flesh to the will of the Father, being the Father and the Son—

"The Father, because he was conceived by the power of God; and the Son, because of the flesh; thus becoming the Father and Son—

"And they are one God, yea, the very Eternal Father of heaven and of earth.

"And thus the flesh becoming subject to the Spirit, or the Son to the Father, being one God, suffereth temptation, and yieldeth not to temptation, but suffereth himself to be mocked, and scourged, and cast out, and disowned by his people." (Mosiah 15:1-5)

Jesus Christ applies to Himself both "Son" and "Father". He said to the brother of Jared: "Behold, I am Jesus Christ. I am the Father and the Son." (Ether 3:14)

Scriptures that refer to God as the Father of

Heavens and earth signify that God is the Maker, the organizer, the creator of heavens and earth. The prophet Joseph Smith explained:

"The word create came from the word Baurau, which does not mean to create out of nothing; it means to organize; the same as a man would organize materials and build a ship. Hence we infer that God had materials to organize the world out of chaos—chaotic matter, which is element, and in which dwells all the glory. Element had an existence from the time he had. The pure principles of element are principles which can never be destroyed; they may be organized and reorganized, but not destroyed. They had no beginning and can have no end." (DPJS, 126)

Elder James E. Talmage has written,

"The Father operated in the work of creation through the Son, who thus became the executive through whom the will, commandment, or word of the Father was put into effect.... The part taken by Jesus Christ in the creation, a part so prominent as to justify our calling Him the Creator, is set forth in many scriptures. The author of the Epistle to the Hebrews...

[wrote,] "God, who at sundry times and in divers manners spake in time past unto the fathers by the prophets, hath in these last days spoken unto us by his Son, whom he hath appointed heir of all things, by whom also he made the worlds." Paul is even more explicit in his letter to the Colossians, wherein, speaking of Jesus the Son, he says: "For by him were all things created, that are in heaven, and that are in earth, visible and invisible, whether they be thrones, or dominions, or principalities, or powers: all things were created by him, and for him: and he is before all things, and by him all things consist." (*Jesus the Christ*, p.33; See also Heb.1:1-2 and Col. 1:16-17)

Jehovah, who is Jesus Christ, the Son of Elohim, is called the Father and even the very Eternal Father of Heaven and of earth. Isaiah wrote that Jesus Christ is "the Mighty God, the everlasting Father." (Isaiah 9:6)

To His faithful followers in the present dispensation, our Lord said: "Fear not, little children, for you are mine, and I have overcome the world, and you are of them that my Father hath given me." (D&C 50:41)

In a revelation to Emma Smith, the Lord addressed

the woman as "my daughter, for verily I say unto you, all those who receive my gospel are sons and daughters in my Kingdom." (D&C 25:1)

By obedience to the gospel men may be sons of God, both as sons of the Savior and through him as sons of the Father. To Hyrum Smith the Lord said: "Behold I am Jesus Christ, the Son of God. I am the life and light of the the world. I am the same who came unto mine own and mine own received me not; but verily, verily, I say unto you that as many as received me, to them will I give power to become the sons of God, even to them that believe on my name." (D&C 11:28-30)

The relationship between Jesus Christ as the Father and those who comply with the requirements of His Gospel as his children, were given by Abinadi centuries before our Lord's birth in the flesh: "And now I say unto you, who shall declare his generation? Behold, I say unto you, that when his soul has been made an offering for sin he shall see his seed. And now what say ye? And who shall be his seed? Behold I say unto you, that whosoever has heard the words of the prophets, yea, all the holy prophets who have prophesied concerning the coming of the Lord—I say unto you, that all those who have hearkened unto their words, and believed that the Lord would redeem his people, and have looked forward to that day for a remission of their sins, I say unto you, that these are his seed, or they are the heirs of the Kingdom of God. For these are they whose sins he has borne; these are they for whom he has died, to redeem them from their transgressions. And now, are they not his seed? Yea, and are not the prophets, every one that has opened his mouth to prophesy, that has not fallen into transgression, I mean all the holy prophets ever since the world began? I say unto you that they are his seed." (Mosiah 15:10-13)

Jesus Christ is also the Father by divine investiture of authority. The Father placed his name upon the Son; and Jesus spoke and ministered in and through the Father's name—His words and acts were and are those of the Father.

The following is an example of that truth as presented in a doctrinal exposition by The First Presidency and the Twelve;

"John, was visited by an angel who ministered and spoke in the name of Jesus Christ. As we read: "The Revelation of Jesus Christ, which God gave unto him, to shew unto his servants things which must shortly come to pass; and he sent and signified it by his angel unto his servant John" (Revelation 1:1). John was about to worship the angelic being who spoke in the name of the Lord Jesus Christ, but was forbidden: "And I John saw these things, and heard them. And when I had heard and seen, I fell down to worship before the feet of the angel which shewed me these things. Then saith he unto me, See thou do it not: for I am thy fellowservant, and of thy brethren the prophets, and of them which keep the sayings of this book: worship God" (Rev. 22:8, 9). And then the angel continued to speak as though he were the Lord Himself: "And, behold, I come quickly; and my reward is with me, to give every man according as his work shall be. I am Alpha and Omega, the beginning and the end, the first and the last. (verses 12, 13.)" (The Father and the Son: A doctrinal Exposition by The First Presidency and the Twelve, June 30, 1916.)

The resurrected savior had placed his name upon the angel sent to John. The angel spoke in the first person and said: "I come quickly, I am Alpha and Omega."

In that great high priestly prayer offered by the Savior just prior to his entrance into Gethsemane, Jesus called upon the Father in behalf of his Apostles and those who would accept and abide in the Gospel, and on this occasion he uttered that oft repeated declaration: "And this is life eternal, that they might know thee the only true God, and Jesus Christ, whom thou hast sent." (IV, John 17:3)

"It is the first principle of the Gospel to know for a certainty the character of God, and to know that we may converse with him as one man converses with another, and that he was once a man like us, Yea, that God himself, the Father of us all, dwelt on an earth, the same as Jesus Christ himself did: And I will show it from the Bible," said the prophet Joseph Smith. (DPJS, 32)

The Lord Jesus Christ revealed to Moses: "...There is no end to my works, neither to my words. "For behold, this is my work and my glory—to bring to pass the immortality and eternal life of man." (Moses 1:38-39)

The Savior revealed to the Prophet Joseph Smith and to Sidney Rigdon the pathway to Celestial Glory which was to come through priesthood ordinances and rightful living on the part of the individual.

"This is the testimony of the gospel of Christ concerning them who shall come forth in the resurrection of the just—

"They are they who received the testimony of Jesus, and believed on his name and were baptized after the manner of his burial, being buried in the water in his name, and this according to the commandment which he has given—

"That by keeping the commandments they might be washed and cleansed from all their sins and receive the Holy Spirit by the laying on of the hands of him who is ordained and sealed unto this power;

"And who overcome by faith, and are sealed by the Holy Spirit of promise, which the Father sheds forth upon all those who are just and true.

"They are they who are the church of the Firstborn.

"They are they into whose hands the Father has given all things—

"They are they who are priests and kings, who have received of his fullness, and of his glory;

And are priests of the Most High, after the order of Melchizedek, which was after the order of Enoch, which was after the order of the Only Begotten Son.

"Wherefore, as it is written, they are gods, even the sons of God—

"Wherefore, all things are theirs, whether life or death, or things present, or things to come, all are theirs and they are Christ's, and Christ is God's.

"And they shall overcome all things." (D&C 76:50-60)

On May 4, 1842, the prophet Joseph Smith conferred the Holy Endowment upon seven of his brethren, for the first time in this The Dispensation of the Fullness of Times. He had been given the Endowment by Revelation from the Lord Jesus Christ.. The prophet said to these brethren: "Your Endowment is to prepare you to overcome all things." (DPJS, 148)

At the laying of the Northeast cornerstone of the Salt Lake Temple, President Brigham Young remarked: "Let me give you the definition in brief. Your endowment is to receive all those ordinances in the House of the Lord, which are necessary for you, after you have departed from this life, to enable you to walk back to the presence of the Father, passing the angels who stand as sentinels, being enabled to give them the key words, the signs and tokens, pertaining to the Holy Priesthood, and gain your eternal exaltation in spite of earth and hell." (JD 2:31)

Through temple ordinances men may come to know God, and receive the keys, powers, etc. associated with Godhood and with immortality and Eternal Life. The prophet explained Eternal Life when he said:

"Here, then, is eternal life—to know the only wise and true God; and you have got to learn how to be gods yourselves, and to be kings and priests to God, the same as all gods have done before you, namely, by going from one small degree to another, and from a small capacity to a great one; from grace to grace, from exaltation to exaltation, until you attain to the resurrection of the dead, and are able to dwell in ever-lasting burnings, and to sit in glory, as do those who sit enthroned in everlasting power." (DPJS, 41)

In section 132 of the Doctrine and Covenants is recorded a revelation revealing the pathway to Godhood. In it the Lord said: "I am the Lord thy God; and I give unto you this commandment—that no man shall come unto the Father but by me or by my word, which is my law, saith the Lord."

"...If a man marry a wife by my word, which is my law, and by the new and everlasting covenant, and it is sealed unto them by the Holy Spirit of promise, by him who is anointed, unto whom I have appointed this power and the keys of this priesthood; and it shall be said unto them—Ye shall come forth in the first resur-rection; and if it be after the first resurrection, in the next resurrection; and shall inherit thrones, kingdoms, principalities, and powers, dominions, all heights and depths-then shall it be written in the Lamb's Book of Life, that he shall commit no murder whereby to shed innocent blood, and if ye abide in my covenant, and commit no murder whereby to shed innocent blood, it shall be done unto them in all things whatsoever my servant hath put upon them, in time, and through all eternity; and shall be of full force when they are out of the world; and they shall pass by the angels, and the gods, which are set there, to their exaltation and glory in all things, as hath been sealed upon their heads, which glory shall be a fullness and a continuation of the seeds forever and ever.

"Then shall they be gods, because they have no end; therefore shall they be from everlasting to ever-lasting, because they continue; then shall they be above all, because all things are subject unto them. Then shall they be gods, because they have all power, and the angels are subject unto them.

"Verily, verily, I say unto you, except ye abide my law ye cannot attain to this glory.

"For strait is the gate, and narrow the way that lead-eth unto the exaltation and continuation of the lives, and few there be that find it, because ye receive me not in the world neither do ye know me.

"But if ye receive me in the world, then shall ye know me, and shall receive your exaltation; that where I am ye shall be also.

"This is eternal lives—to know the only wise and true God, and Jesus Christ, whom he hath sent." (D&C 132:12, 19-24)

The prophet Joseph Smith counseled: "Hold out to the end, and we shall be resurrected and become Gods, and reign in Celestial Kingdoms, principalities, and Eternal Dominions." (DPJS, 137)

President George Q. Cannon said, "It is a glorious thing...to know that our religion is true and given us from God and that in obedience to it we may attain to the exalted position occupied by Him and our Lord and Savior Jesus Christ.... We are of the race of God, the sons and daughters of a King. (GT, Vol 1, p.110)

President Cannon gave extended meaning to the great truths that had been revealed. These are his words: "It is God's design to make us priests and kings, not to have an empty title, not to sit upon thrones without power but to be actually and really priests and kings. The promise is that all things that He hath shall be given unto us. We will be His heirs; we will be (if I may use the term without irreverence) co-partners with Him in all this power and authority... (GT, Vol 1, p.112)

He referred to the fact that to the increase of the Lord's Government there is no end and declared that this would also be true of Celestial Families.

"The godlike power has been given us here on the earth to bear and perpetuate our own species. Shall this power, which brings so much joy, peace and happiness, be confined and limited to this short life? It is folly to talk about such a thing; common sense teaches us better. It teaches that we have been organized not for time alone, that we have been endowed as we are in the image of God not for thirty, forty, fifty, seventy or a hundred years but as eternal beings, exercising our endowments and functions for all eternity, if we live faithful or take a course that God approves. Therefore, there is great sense, beauty and godliness in the idea that God taught Abraham with respect to his posterity becoming as numerous as the stars of the firmament....

"We look forward to the time when this earth will be redeemed from corruption and cleansed by fire, when there shall be a new heaven and a new earth and when the Saints shall possess their native inheritance purified from sin, redeemed from corruption, with the power of Satan curtailed and when we shall be able to increase and multiply and fill this earth, go to other earths and carry on the work of emigration through the endless ages of eternity. He has revealed to us that these relationships that are so tender and that make life so delightful will exist beyond the grave. Wife will be united to husband. Children will be united to parents. The family relationship will exist in eternity, and the glory of a man and a woman will be in dwelling in the midst of their posterity and seeing that posterity increase." (GT, Vol 1, p.116)

Jesus Christ is the Heir of our Heavenly Father's family and holds the keys over all this world. No one ever lived on this earth that has exerted the same influence upon the souls of men and upon the destinies of the world as He did.

He is the Only Begotten Son of God in the flesh; He is the creator of the world; He atoned for Adam's transgression; He is the sacrifice for the sins of all the world; He laid down His life to redeem all mankind; He has risen again and has ascended to the Father; He has brought to pass the immortality and eternal life for all mankind. There is no other name under heaven, save it be Jesus Christ, whereby we must be saved.

The pathway to Godhood, will not be accomplished in this mortal life. This truth is expressed by the Prophet in these words.

"When you climb up a ladder, you must begin at the bottom, and ascend step by step, until you arrive at the top; and so it is with the principles of the gospel— you must begin with the first, and go on until you learn all the principles of exaltation. But it will be a great while after you have passed through the veil before you will have learned them. It is not all to be comprehended in this world; it will be a great work to learn our salvation and exaltation even beyond the grave." (DPJS, 138)

When we do attain salvation and exaltation, we shall be in association with and in subjection to Jesus Christ, who is the God of this world.

CHAPTER TWO
THE MIRACLE OF THE ATONEMENT

The atonement of the Lord Jesus Christ is the most important single event that has occurred since the days of the creation.

"The atonement...was prepared from the foundation of the world for all mankind, which ever were since the fall of Adam, or who are, or who ever shall be, even unto the end of the world," according to King Benjamin. (Mosiah 4:7)

The prophet Joseph Smith taught that "The fundamental principles of our religion are the testimony of the Apostles and Prophets, concerning Jesus Christ, that He died, was buried, and rose again the third day, and ascended into heaven; and all other things which pertain to our religion are only appendages to it." (DPJS, 272)

The prophet in recording the vision of the glories wrote of the mission of Christ in these words: "And this is the gospel, the glad tidings, which the voice out of the heavens bore record unto us—That he came into the world, even Jesus, to be crucified for the world, and to bear the sins of the world, and to sanctify the world, and to cleanse it from all unrighteousness; That through him all might be saved whom the Father had put into his power and made by him." (D&C 76:40-42)

The resurrected Lord said to the Nephites: "Behold I have given unto you my gospel, and this is the gospel which I have given unto you—that I came into the world to do the will of my Father, because my Father sent me. And my Father sent me that I might be lifted up upon the cross." (3 Ne. 27:13-14)

Lehi explained the fall and the redemption of mankind when he said: "Adam fell that men might be; and men are, that they might have joy, and the Messiah cometh in the fullness of time, that he may redeem the children of men from the fall." (2 Ne. 2:25-26)

Lehi expanded on the redemption of the sons and daughters of Adam and Eve: "...redemption cometh in and through the Holy Messiah; for he is full of grace and truth. Behold, he offereth himself a sacrifice for sin, to answer the ends of the law, unto all those who have a broken heart and a contrite spirit; and unto none else can the ends of the law be answered. Wherefore, how great the importance to make these things known unto the inhabitants of the earth, that they may know that there is no flesh that can dwell in the presence of God, save it be through the merits, and mercy, and grace of the Holy Messiah, who layeth down his life according to the flesh, and taketh it again by the power of the Spirit, that he may bring to pass the resurrection of the dead, being the first that should rise. Wherefore, he is the firstfruits unto God, inasmuch as he shall make intercession for all the children of men; and they that believe in him shall be saved." (2 Ne. 2:6-9)

President John Taylor and Elder Bruce R. McConkie have explained what would have happened if there had been no atonement. First, from Elder McConkie: "If there had been no atonement of Christ (there having been a fall of Adam!), then the whole plan and purpose connected with the creation of man would have come to naught. If there had been no atonement, temporal death would have remained forever, and there never would have been a resurrection. The body would have remained forever in the grave, and the spirit would have stayed in a spirit prison to all eternity. If there had been no atonement, there never would have been spiritual or eternal life for any persons. Neither mortals nor spirits could have been cleansed from sin, and all the spirit hosts of heaven would have wound up as devils, angels to a devil, that is, as sons of perdition." (MD, 63)

President Taylor taught that "If it were not for the atonement of Jesus Christ, the sacrifice He made, all the human family would have to lie in the grave throughout eternity without any hope. But God having provided, through the atonement of the Lord Jesus Christ, the medium whereby we can be restored to the bosom and presence of the Father, to participate with Him among the Gods in the eternal worlds—He, having provided for that, has also provided for the resurrection." (JD 22:356) The atonement made by Jesus Christ brought about the resurrection from the dead and restored life.

Jacob, younger brother of Nephi, wrote regarding the plight of mankind if the atonement had not been made: "For as death hath passed upon all men, to fulfil the merciful plan of the great Creator, there must needs be a power of resurrection, and the resurrection must needs come unto man by reason of the fall; and the fall came by reason of transgression; and because man became fallen they were cut off from the presence of the Lord. Wherefore, it must needs be an infinite atonement—save it should be an infinite atonement this corruption could not put on incorruption. Wherefore, the first judgment which came upon man must needs have remained to an endless duration. And if so, this flesh must have laid down to rot and to crumble to its mother earth, to rise no more. O the wisdom of God, his mercy and grace! For behold, if the flesh should rise no more our spirits must become subject to that angel who fell from before the presence of the Eternal God, and became the devil, to rise no more. And our spirits must have become like unto him, and we become devils, angels to a devil, to be shut off from the presence of our God, and to remain with the father of lies, in misery, like unto himself." (2 Ne. 9:6-9)

The fall and the atonement were foreordained and the plan of salvation, known as the gospel of Jesus Christ, was adopted in the heavens before the foundation of the earth. President Joseph Fielding Smith said that "It was appointed [in the Heavens] that Adam, our father, should come to this earth and stand at the head of the whole human family. It was a part of this great plan, that he should partake of the forbidden fruit and fall, thus bringing suffering and death into the world, even for the ultimate good of his children." (DS 1:121) And further, President Smith said "It was also necessary because of Adam's transgression for the Only Begotten Son of the Father to come to redeem the world from Adam's fall. This also was a part of the plan chosen before the earth was made, for Jesus is called the Lamb that was slain from the foundation of the world. He came and redeemed us from the fall— even all the inhabitants of the earth. Not only did he redeem us from Adam's transgression, but he also redeemed us from our own sins, on condition that we obey the laws and ordinances of the gospel." (DS 1:121)

President John Taylor asked "Was it known that man would fall? Yes. We are clearly told that it was understood that man should fall, and it was understood that the penalty of departing from the law would be death, death temporal. And there was a provision made for that. Man was not able to make that provision himself, and hence we are told that it needed the atonement of a God to accomplish this purpose; and the Son of God presented Himself to carry out that object. And when He presented Himself for this position He was accepted by His Father.... So Jesus offered Himself. Now, man could not have done that. Man could do all that he is capable of doing. But there was an eternal law of God violated and it needed an eternal, infinite sacrifice to atone therefor; and Jesus offered Himself as that sacrifice to atone for the sins of the world; and hence it is written, He was the Lamb slain from before the foundation of the world." (JD 22:300)

President Brigham Young taught that "A divine debt has been contracted by the children, and the Father demands recompense. He says to His children on this earth, who are in sin and transgression, it is impossible for you to pay this debt; I have prepared a sacrifice; I will send my Only Begotten Son to pay this divine debt. Was it necessary then that Jesus should die? Do we understand why He should sacrifice His life? The idea that the Son of God, who never committed sin, should sacrifice His life is unquestionably preposterous to the minds of many in the Christian world. But the fact exists that the Father, the Divine Father, whom we serve, the God of the Universe, the God and Father of our Lord Jesus Christ, and the Father of our spirits, provided this sacrifice and sent His Son to die for us; and it is also a great fact that the Son came to do the will of the Father, and that He has paid the debt, in fulfillment of the Scripture which says, 'He was the Lamb slain from the foundation of the world.'...Unless God provides a Savior to pay this debt it can never be paid. Can all the wisdom of the world devise means by which we can be redeemed, and return to the presence of our Father and Elder Brother, and dwell with holy angels and celestial beings? No; it is beyond the power and wisdom of the inhabitants of the earth that now live, or that ever did or ever will live, to prepare or create a sacrifice that will pay this divine debt. But God provided it, and His Son has paid it, and we, each and every one, can now receive the truth and be saved in the kingdom of God." (JD 14:71-72)

The Prophet Joseph Smith explained that the Lord prepared a sacrifice in the gift of His Only Begotten Son and that through the shedding of the blood of His Only Begotten redemption could be carried out. Here is his explanation: "That man was not able himself to erect a system or plan with power sufficient to free him from a destruction which awaited him is evident from the fact that God...prepared a sacrifice in the gift of His own Son who would be sent in due time, to prepare a way, or open a door through which man might enter in to the Lord's presence, whence he had been cast out for disobedience. From time to time these glad tidings were sounded in the ears of men in different ages of the world down to the time of Messiah's coming. By faith in this atonement or plan of redemption, Abel offered to God a sacrifice that was accepted, which was the firstlings of the flock. It must be—shedding the blood of the Only Begotten to atone for man; for this was the plan of redemption; and without the shedding of blood was no remission." (DPJS, 80)

The miracle of the atonement is in a manner to us incomprehensible and inexplicable, President John

Taylor said, "[Christ] bore the weight of the sins of the whole world; not only of Adam, but of his posterity; and in doing that, opened the kingdom of heaven, not only to all believers and all who obeyed the law of God, but to more than one-half of the human family who die before they come to years of maturity, as well as to the heathen, who, having died without law, will, through His mediation, be resurrected without law, and be judged without law, and thus participate, according to their capacity, works, and worth in the blessings of His Atonement.... He in His own person bore the sins of all, and atoned for them by the sacrifice of Himself, so there came upon Him the weight and agony of ages and generations, the indescribable agony consequent upon this great sacrificial atonement wherein He bore the sins of the world, and suffered in His own person the consequences of an eternal law of God broken by man. Hence His profound grief, His indescribable anguish, His overpowering torture, all experienced in the submission to the eternal fiat of Jehovah and the requirements of an inexorable law." (MA, p. 148-150, Published in 1882)

President Joseph Fielding Smith discoursed upon the profound grief, the indescribable anguish, and his overpowering torture as presented by President Taylor. Said he: "Now think of the Savior carrying a burden in some way which I cannot understand but which I know to be true, which I am sure, you do not understand, a united burden of the sins of all those who have sinned and who have repented of their sins. He carried the burden of that upon himself and paid the price through suffering. You know a great many people think that the great suffering the Savior had was having the nails driven through his hands and in his feet and being left to die on a cross. As excruciating as that was and as severe as the pain had to be, others have suffered that, thousands. It was a way of capital punishment used by the Romans. Men have been tortured, but that was the least of the suffering of the Son of God. His suffering was greater before he ever went to the cross, when he prayed to his Father that the cup might pass he was not thinking of the nails in his hands and his feet and hanging on the cross. It was the torment of his soul in some mysterious way in which he was benefiting you and me and all who are willing to accept him as their Redeemer and keep his commandments. It was the united burden of the sins which we would have had to pay for if it could have been possible and if there had been no atonement. He paid that price. It was before he ever went to the cross that the blood oozed from the pores of his body and that the great anguish came upon him which was so terrific. When I think of his being willing to carry that burden of sin to relieve us, I feel that I want to keep his commandments. I want to love him..." (CR, October 1969, p. 57)

King Benjamin testified, long before Christ's birth, of the Savior's ministry: "And lo, he shall suffer temptations, and pain of body, hunger, thirst, and fatigue, even more than man can suffer, except it be unto death; for behold, blood cometh from every pore, so great shall be his anguish for the wickedness and the abominations of his people." (Mosiah 3:7)

Another account of this was given by the Lord to Joseph Smith when He said: "For behold, I, God, have suffered these things for all, that they might not suffer if they would repent; But if they would not repent they must suffer even as I; Which suffering caused myself, even God, the greatest of all, to tremble because of pain, and to bleed at every pore, and to suffer both body and spirit—and would that I might not drink the bitter cup, and shrink—Nevertheless, glory be to the Father, and I partook and finished my preparations unto the children of men." (D&C 19:16-19)

Amulek taught that there had to be an infinite eternal sacrifice. Said he: "I do know that Christ shall come among the children of men, to take upon him the transgressions of his people, and that he shall atone for the sins of the world; for the Lord God hath spoken it. For it is expedient that an atonement should be made; for according to the great plan of the Eternal God there must be an atonement made, or else all mankind must unavoidably perish; yea, all are hardened; yea, all are fallen and are lost, and must perish except it be through the atonement which it is expedient should be made. For it is expedient that there should be a great and last sacrifice; yea, not a sacrifice of man, neither of beast, neither of any manner of fowl; for it shall not be a human sacrifice; but it must be an infinite and eternal sacrifice. Now there is not any man that can sacrifice his own blood which will atone for the sins of another.... Therefore there can be nothing which is short of an infinite atonement which will suffice for the sins of the world." (Alma 34:8-12)

Elder McConkie said "When the prophets speak of an infinite atonement, they mean just that. Its effects cover all men, the earth itself and all forms of life thereon, and reach out into the endless expanses of eternity." (MD, 64)

President Joseph Fielding Smith taught that the atonement of Christ through the shedding of His blood redeemed every living thing, even the earth itself. And he said, "I believe in Jesus Christ as the Son of God and the Only Begotten Son of the Father in the flesh: that he came into the world as the Redeemer, as the Savior; and through his death, through his ministry, the shedding of his blood, he has brought to pass redemption from death to all men, to all creatures—not alone to man, but to every living thing, and even to this earth itself, upon which we stand, for we are informed through the revelations that it too shall receive the resurrection and come forth to be crowned as a celestial body, and to be the abode of celestial beings eternally." (DS 1:138)

The Prophet Joseph Smith when speaking of the power of the Savior said: "As the Father hath power in himself, so hath the Son power in himself, to lay down his life and take it again, so he has a body of his own." (DPJS, 40)

Elder McConkie explained why the Savior was able to lay down his life and to take it up again. Said he: "Christ is the only person ever to be born in the world who had power to bring to pass the resurrection of himself or anyone else and to atone for the sins of any living being. This is because he had life in himself; he had the power of immortality by divine inheritance. The atonement came by the power of God and not of man, and to understand it one must believe that our Lord was literally the Son of God (an immortal Personage) and of Mary (a mortal woman). From his mother he inherited mortality, the power to lay down his life, to die, to permit body and spirit to separate. From his Father he inherited the power of immortality, the power to keep body and spirit together, or voluntarily having permitted them to separate, the power to unite them again in the resurrected state." (MD, 64)

Our Lord and Savior Jesus Christ is the center of all things both in heaven and on earth. Nephi placed great emphasis to his people on the Savior's mission. He said: "...we talk of Christ, we rejoice in Christ, we preach of Christ, we prophesy of Christ, and we write according to our prophecies, that our children may know to what source they may look for a remission of their sins.... And now behold, my people...the words which I have spoken...are sufficient to teach any man the right way; for the right way is to believe in Christ." (2 Ne. 25:26, 28)

The principle of justice, mercy, and repentance—all of which relate to the atonement, were the subject of Alma's discourse to his son Corianton. He said: "Therefore, according to justice, the plan of redemption could not be brought about, only on conditions of repentance of men in this probationary state, yea, this preparatory state; for except it were for these conditions, mercy could not take effect except it should destroy the work of justice. Now the work of justice could not be destroyed; if so, God would cease to be God. And thus we see that all mankind were fallen, and they were in the grasp of justice; yea, the justice of God, which consigned them forever to be cut off from his presence. And now, the plan of mercy could not be brought about except an atonement should be made; therefore God himself atoneth for the sins of the world, to bring about the plan of mercy, to appease the demands of justice, that God might be a perfect, just God, and a merciful God also. Now, repentance could not come unto men except there were a punishment, which also was eternal as the life of the soul should be, affixed opposite to the plan of happiness, which was as eternal also as the life of the soul. Now, how could a man repent except he should sin? How could he sin if there was no law? How could there be a law save there was a punishment?... But there is a law given, and a punishment affixed, and a repentance granted; which repentance, mercy claimeth; otherwise, justice claimeth the creature and executeth the law, and the law inflicteth the punishment; if not so, the works of justice would be destroyed, and God would cease to be God. But God ceaseth not to be God, and mercy claimeth the penitent, and mercy cometh because of the atonement; and the atonement bringeth to pass the resurrection of the dead; and the resurrection of the dead bringeth back men into the presence of God; and thus they are restored into his presence, to be judged according to their works, according to the law and justice. For behold, justice exerciseth all his demands, and also mercy claimeth all which is her own; and thus, none but the truly penitent are saved." (Alma 42:13-17, 22-24)

In summary:

1. The atonement was prepared from before the foundation of the world.
2. The atonement provided that Christ should come to suffer, to die, to be buried, to rise again and to ascend into heaven.
3. As in Adam all die even so in Christ shall all be made alive.
4. If there had been no atonement, all the human family would have remained in the grave and would have become subject to the devil.

5. Both the fall and the atonement were foreordained. The Savior became known as the lamb that was slain before the foundation of the world.

6. A divine debt had been contracted through the fall and required a God to pay the debt.

7. There is nothing short of an infinite and eternal sacrifice, even the shedding of the blood of Christ, that could bring about the redemption of mankind.

8. Through Christ's atonement every living thing, even the earth itself, will be redeemed.

9. Christ suffered profound grief, indescribable anguish, overpowering torture, and shed great drops of blood.

10. Christ was the son of God, an immortal personage, and of Mary a mortal person—therefore he could lay down his life and he could take it up again.

11. The principles of justice, mercy, and repentance make possible that man may gain exaltation in the celestial kingdom by obeying the laws of the gospel.

12. "[Christ] doeth not anything save it be for the benefit of the world; for he loveth the world, even that he layeth down his own life that he may draw all men to him. Wherefore, he commandeth none that they shall not partake of His salvation."

(2 Ne. 26:24) His message is to one and all alike, "Come unto me." Finally, as we think upon the greatness of his atonement in our behalf, let us recall the words of the hymn by Charles H. Gabriel: "I stand all amazed at the love Jesus offers me, confused at the grace that so fully he proffers me. I tremble to know that for me he was crucified. That for me, a sinner, He suffered, He bled and died. Oh, it is wonderful that he should care for me enough to die for me! Oh, it is wonderful, wonderful to me!" (Hymns of the Church of Jesus Christ of Latter-day Saints, pp.193-194)

Chapter Three
The Reality Of
Christ's Resurrection

The reality of the resurrection of the Lord Jesus Christ was recorded in the meridian of time by Matthew, Mark, Luke, and John. Each writer gave a personal account of Christ's having risen from the dead.

Paul likewise gave his testimony of the risen Lord and declared further that on one occasion the Lord was seen of above 500 brethren at once.

The scriptures (Book of Mormon) testify that Christ appeared to the people of the American continent at which time he had them feel the print of the nails in his hands and feet and the wound in his side. These same scriptures also testify that He appeared to the people known as the Ten Lost Tribes of Israel (see 3 Ne. 16:3). Christ has also appeared to apostles and prophets in these latter days.

Mary Magdalene was the first to learn that Christ had risen from the dead. John recorded: "The first day of the week cometh Mary Magdalene early, when it was yet dark, unto the sepulchre, and seeth the stone taken away from the sepulchre, and two angels sitting thereon.

"Then she runneth, and cometh to Simon Peter, and to the other disciple, whom Jesus loved, and saith unto them, they have taken away the Lord out of the sepulchre, and we know not where they have laid him.

"Peter therefore went forth, and that other disciple, and came to the sepulchre.

"So they ran both together: and the other disciple did outrun Peter, and came first to the sepulchre.

"And he stooping down, and looking in, saw the linen clothes lying; yet went he not in.

"Then cometh Simon Peter following him, and went into the sepulchre, and seeth the linen clothes lie, And the napkin, that was about his head, not lying with the linen clothes, but wrapped together in a place by itself.

"Then went in also that other disciple, which came first to the sepulchre, and he saw, and believed.

"For as yet they knew not the scripture, that he must rise again from the dead.

"Then the disciples went away again unto their own home." (IV, John 20:1-10)

Jesus' appearance to Mary near the sepulchre is one of most soul stirring and a most beautiful experience yet recorded. "...Mary stood without at the sepulchre weeping: and as she wept, she stooped down, and looked into the sepulchre,

"And seeth two angels in white sitting, the one at the head, and the other at the feet, where the body of Jesus had lain.

"And they say unto her, Woman, why weepest thou? She saith unto them, Because they have taken away my Lord, and I know not where they have laid him.

"And when she had thus said, she turned herself back, and saw Jesus standing, and knew not that it was Jesus.

"Jesus saith unto her, Woman, why weepest thou? Whom seekest thou? She, supposing him to be the gardener, saith unto him, Sir, if thou have borne him hence, tell me where thou hast laid him, and I will take him away.

"Jesus saith unto her, Mary. She turned herself, and saith unto him, Rabboni; which is to say, Master.

"Jesus saith unto her, Hold me not; for I am not yet ascended to my Father: but go to my brethren, and say unto them, I ascend unto my Father, and your Father; and to my God, and your God." (IV, John 20:11-17)

Following this, Jesus appeared to other women. Matthew recorded: "And as they went to tell his disciples, behold, Jesus met them, saying, All hail! And they came and held him by the feet, and worshipped him.

"Then said Jesus unto them, Be not afraid; go tell my brethren that they go into Galilee, and there shall they see me." (IV, Matthew 28:7-9)

Then Mary and the other women "...returned from the sepulchre, and told all these things unto the eleven, and to all the rest.

"It was Mary Magdalene, and Joanna, and Mary the mother of James, and other women who were with them, which told these things unto the apostles. And their words seemed to them as idle tales, and they believed them not." (IV, Luke 24:8-10)

Jesus appeared to two of his disciples on the road to Emmaus and after visiting with them revealed to them who he was:

"...Two of them went that same day to a village called Emmaus, which was from Jerusalem three-score furlongs.

"And they talked together of all these things which had happened.

"And it came to pass, that while they communed together, and reasoned, Jesus himself drew near, and went with them.

"But their eyes were holden or covered, that they could not know him.

"And he said unto them, What manner of communications are these which ye have one with another, as ye walk and are sad?

"And one of them, whose name was Cleopas, answering, said unto him, Art thou only a stranger in Jerusalem, and hast not known the things which are come to pass there in these days?

"And he said unto them, What things? And they said unto him, Concerning Jesus of Nazareth, who was a prophet mighty in deed and word before God and all the people;

"And how the chief priests and our rulers delivered him to be condemned to death, and have crucified him.

"But we trusted that it had been he who should have redeemed Israel. And besides all this, today is the third day since these things were done;

"Yea, and certain women also of our company made us astonished, who were early at the sepulchre; and when they found not his body, they came, saying, that they had also seen a vision of angels; who said that he was alive.

"And certain of them who were with us, went to the sepulchre, and found it even so as the women had said, but him they saw not.

"Then he said unto them, O fools, and slow of heart to believe all that the prophets have spoken!

"Ought not Christ to have suffered these things, and to enter into his glory?

"And beginning at Moses and all the prophets, he expounded unto them in all the scriptures the things concerning himself.

"And they drew nigh unto the village whither they went: and he made as though he would have gone further.

"But they constrained him, saying, Abide with us; for it is toward evening, and the day is far spent. "And he went in to tarry with them.

"And it came to pass, as he sat at meat with them, he took bread, and blessed it, and brake, and gave to them.

"And their eyes were opened, and they knew him; and he was taken up out of their sight.

"And they said one to another, Did not our heart burn within us, while he talked with us by the way, and while he opened to us the scriptures?" (IV, Luke 24:12-31)

Christ's first appearance to the ten apostles was recorded by John:

"Then the same day at evening, being the first day of the week, when the doors were shut where the disciples were assembled for fear of the Jews, came Jesus and stood in the midst, and saith unto them, Peace be unto you.

"And when he had so said, he shewed unto them his hands and his side. Then were the disciples glad, when they saw the Lord.

"Then said Jesus to them again, Peace be unto you: as my Father hath sent me, even so send I you.

"And when he had said this, he breathed on them, and saith unto them, Receive ye the Holy Ghost:

"Whosoever sins ye remit, they are remitted unto them; and whosoever sins ye retain, they are retained." (IV, John 20:19-23)

Christ's second appearance was likewise recorded by John:

"But Thomas, one of the twelve, called Didymus, was not with them when Jesus came.

"The other disciples therefore said unto him, we have seen the Lord. But he said unto them, Except I shall see in his hands the print of the nails, and put my finger into the print of the nails, and thrust my hand into his side, I will not believe.

"And after eight days again his disciples were within, and Thomas with them: then came Jesus, the doors being shut, and stood in the midst, and said, Peace unto you.

"Then saith he to Thomas, Reach hither thy finger, and behold my hands; and reach hither thy hand, and thrust it into my side: and be not faithless, but believing.

"And Thomas answered and said unto him, My Lord and my God.

"Jesus saith unto him, Thomas, because thou hast seen me, thou hast believed: blessed are they that have not seen, and yet have believed." (IV, John 20:24-29)

"After these things Jesus showed himself again to his disciples at the Sea of Tiberias; and on this wise showed he himself. There were together Simon Peter, and Thomas called Didymus, and Nathaniel of Cana in Galilee, and the two sons of Zebedee, and two other of his disciples. Simon Peter saith unto them, I go a fishing. They say unto him, We also go with thee. They went forth, and entered into a ship immediately; and that night they caught nothing. But when the morning was now come, Jesus stood on the shore; but the disciples knew not that it was Jesus. Then Jesus saith unto them, Children, have ye any meat? They answered him, No. And he saith unto them, cast the net on the right side of the ship, and ye shall find. They cast therefore, and now they were not able to draw it for the multitude of fishes, therefore that disciple whom Jesus loved saith unto Peter, it is the Lord. Now when Simon Peter heard that it was the Lord, he girt his fisher's coat unto him, (for he was naked,) and did cast himself into the sea, and the other disciples came in a little ship: (for they were not far from land, but as it were two hundred cubits,) dragging the net with fishes. As soon then as they come to land, they saw a fire of coals there, and fishes laid thereon, and bread. Jesus saith unto them, bring of the fish of which ye have now caught. Simon Peter went up, and drew the net to land full of great fishes, an hundred and fifty and three: and for all there were so many, yet was not the net broken. Jesus saith unto them, come and dine. And none of the disciples durst ask him, who art thou? Knowing that it was the Lord. Jesus then cometh, and taketh bread, and giveth them, and fish likewise. This is now the third time that Jesus shewed himself to his disciples, after that he was risen from the dead. (IV, John 21:1-14)

Jesus questioned Peter and invited him to feed his

sheep. "So when they had dined, Jesus saith to Simon Peter, Simon, son of Jonas, lovest thou me more than these? He saith unto him, Yea, Lord; thou knowest that I love thee. He saith unto him, Feed my lambs.

"He saith unto him again the second time, Simon, son of Jonas, lovest thou me? He saith unto him, Yea, Lord; thou knowest that I love thee. He saith unto him, Feed my sheep.

"He saith unto him the third time, Simon, son of Jonas, lovest thou me? Peter was grieved because he said unto him the third time, Lovest thou me? And he said unto him, Lord, thou knowest all things; thou knowest that I love thee. Jesus saith unto him, Feed my sheep.

"Verily, verily, I say unto thee, when you wast young, thou girdest thyself, and walkest wither thou wouldest: but when thou shalt be old, thou shalt stretch forth thy hands, and another shall gird thee, and carry thee wither thou wouldest not.

"This spake he, signifying by what death he should glorify God. And when he had spoken this, he saith unto him, Follow me." (IV, John 21:15-19)

Peter asks about John the Beloved and what he should do. "Then Peter, turning about, seeth the disciple whom Jesus loved following;...

"Peter seeing him saith to Jesus, Lord, and what shall this man do?

"Jesus saith unto him, If I will that he tarry till I come, what is that to thee? Follow thou me.

"Then went this saying abroad among the brethren, that that disciple should not die: yet Jesus said not unto him, He shall not die; but, If I will that he tarry till I come, what is that to thee?" (IV, John 21:20-23)

Jesus appeared again in Galilee to his apostles. "Then the eleven disciples went away into Galilee, into a mountain where Jesus had appointed them.

"And when they saw him, they worshipped him: but some doubted.

"And Jesus came and spake unto them, saying, "All power is given unto me in heaven and in earth.

"Go ye therefore, and teach all nations, baptizing them in the name of the Father, and of the Son, and of the Holy Ghost;

"Teaching them to observe all things whatsoever I

have commanded you; and, lo, I am with you always, unto the end of the world." (IV, Matthew 28:15-19)

Jesus ascended into heaven as his apostles stood by on the Mount of Olives. "When they therefore were come together, they asked of him, saying, Lord, wilt thou at this time restore again the kingdom to Israel? And he said unto them, It is not for you to know the times or the seasons, which the Father hath put in his own power. But ye shall receive power, after that the Holy Ghost is come upon you: and ye shall be witnesses unto me both in Jerusalem, and in all Judea, and in Samaria, and the uttermost part of the earth.

"And when he had spoken these things, while they beheld, he was taken up; and a cloud received him out of their sight.

"And while they looked steadfastly toward heaven as he went up, behold, two men stood by them in white apparel;

"Which also said, Ye men of Galilee, why stand ye gazing up into heaven? This same Jesus, which is taken up from you into heaven, shall so come in like manner as ye have seen him go into heaven.

"Then returned they unto Jerusalem from the mount called Olivet, which is from Jerusalem a sabbath day's journey.

"And when they were come in, they went up into an upper room, where abode both Peter, and James, and John, and Andrew, Phillip, and Thomas, Bartholomew, and Matthew, James the son of Alphaeus, and Simon Zelotes, and Judas the brother of James. These all continued with one accord in prayer and supplication, with the women, and Mary the mother of Jesus, and with his brethren. (IV, Acts 1:6-14)

The Apostle Paul also made known other appearances of the Savior after his resurrection:

"...Christ died for our sins according to the scriptures; And that he was buried, and that he rose again the third day according to the scriptures: And that he was seen of Cephas, then of the twelve; after that, he was seen of above five hundred brethren at once; of whom the greater part remain unto this present, but some are fallen asleep. After that, he was seen of James; then of all the apostles. And last of all he was seen of me also, as of one born out of due time." (IV, 1 Cor 15:3-8)

Jesus appeared on the American Continent to 2500 Saints at once as is recorded in III Nephi.

"And it came to pass that in the ending of the thirty and fourth year, behold, I will show unto you that the people of Nephi who were spared, and also those who had been called Lamanites, who had been spared, did have great favors shown unto them, and great blessings poured out upon their heads, insomuch that soon after the ascension of Christ into heaven he did truly manifest himself unto them—

"Showing his body unto them, and ministering unto them;" (3 Nephi 10:18-19)

"And now it came to pass that there were a great multitude gathered together, of the people of Nephi, round about the temple which was in the land Bountiful; and they were marveling and wondering one to another, and were showing one to another the great and marvelous change which had taken place.

"And they were also conversing about this Jesus Christ, of whom the sign had been given concerning his death.

"And it came to pass that while they were thus

conversing one another, they heard a voice as if it came out of heaven; and they cast their eyes round about, for they understood not the voice which they heard; and it was not a harsh voice, neither was it a loud voice; nevertheless, and notwithstanding it being a small voice it did pierce them that did hear to the center, insomuch that there was no part of their frame that it did not cause to quake; yea, it did pierce them to the very soul, and did cause their hearts to burn.

"And it came to pass that again they heard the voice, and they understood it not.

"And again the third time they did hear the voice, and did open their ears to hear it; and their eyes were towards the sound thereof; and they did look steadfastly towards heaven, from whence the sound came.

"And behold, the third time they did understand the voice which they heard; and it said unto them:

"Behold, my Beloved Son, in whom I am well pleased, in whom I have glorified my name—hear ye him.

"And it came to pass, as they understood they cast their eyes up again toward heaven; and behold, they saw a Man descending out of heaven; and he was clothed in a white robe; and he came down and stood in the midst of them; and the eyes of the whole multitude were turned upon him, and they durst not open their mouths, even one to another, and wist not what it meant, for they thought it was an angel that had appeared unto them.

"And it came to pass that he stretched forth his hand and spake unto the people, saying:

"Behold, I am Jesus Christ, whom the prophets testified shall come into the world.

"And behold, I am the light and the life of the world; and I have drunk out of that bitter cup which the Father hath given me, and have glorified the Father in taking upon me the sins of the world, in the which I have suffered the will of the Father in all things from the beginning.

"And it came to pass that when Jesus had spoken these words the whole multitude fell to the earth; for they remembered that it had been prophesied among them that Christ should show himself unto them after his ascension into heaven.

"And it came to pass that the Lord spake unto them saying:

"Arise and come forth unto me, that ye may thrust your hands into my side, and also that ye may feel the prints of the nails in my hands and in my feet, that ye may know that I am the God of Israel, and the God of the whole earth, and have been slain for the sins of the world.

"And it came to pass that the multitude went forth, and thrust their hands into his side, and did feel the prints of the nails in his hands and in his feet; and thus they did do, going forth one by one until they had all gone forth, and did see with their eyes and did feel with their hands, and did know of a surety and did bear record, that it was he, of whom it was written by the prophets, that should come.

"And when they had all gone forth and had witnessed for themselves, they did cry out with one accord, saying:

"Hosanna! Blessed be the name of the Most High God! And they did fall down at the feet of Jesus, and did worship him." (3 Nephi 11:1-17)

Jesus made known to the Nephites that he had other sheep which are not of this land, neither of the land of Jerusalem, neither in any parts of that land round about whither I have been to minister. "For they of whom I speak are they who have not as yet heard my voice: neither have I at any time manifested myself unto them. But I have received a commandment of the Father that I shall go unto them, and they shall hear my voice, and shall be numbered among my sheep, that there may be one fold and one shepherd; therefore I go to show myself unto them...but now I go unto the Father, and also to show myself unto the lost tribes of Israel, for they are not lost unto the Father, for He knoweth whither he hath taken them. (3 Nephi 16:2-3, 17:4)

The greatest event to happen on this earth since the resurrection of Jesus Christ occurred on a beautiful clear day early in the spring of 1820. Joseph Smith saw, in answer to his humble prayer, a pillar of light exactly over his head, above the brightness of the sun which descended gradually until it fell upon him. He saw "two personages, whose brightness and glory defy all description, standing above him in the air." One of them spoke to him calling him by name and said, pointing to the other "This is My Beloved Son, Hear Him." Joseph conversed with the Savior and asked Him which of all the sects was right. The Savior answered his question saying that they were all wrong and that he should not join any of them. (see JSH 1:17-19)

On the sixteenth day of February 1832 Joseph Smith and Sidney Rigdon saw and conversed with the Lord Jesus Christ in the Heavenly vision. Said they "For we saw him, even on the right hand of God; and we heard the voice bearing record that he is the Only Begotten of the Father—that by him, and through him, and of him the worlds are and were created, and the inhabitants thereof are begotten sons and daughters unto God." (D&C 76:23-24) That "this is the testimony, last of all, which we give of him: "That he Lives!" (D&C 76:22)

On April 3, 1836, Joseph Smith and Oliver Cowdery saw the Lord: "The veil was taken from our minds, and the eyes of our understanding were opened. We saw the Lord standing upon the breastwork of the pulpit, before us; and under his feet was a paved work of pure gold, in color like amber. His eyes were as a flame of fire; the hair of his head was white like the pure snow; his countenance shone above the brightness of the sun; and his voice was as the sound of the rushing of great waters, even the voice of Jehovah, saying: I am the first and the last; I am he who liveth, I am he who was slain; I am your advocate with the Father." (D&C 110:1-4)

Many years later, at the turn of the Century, 1898 to be exact, Lorenzo Snow gave his testimony to his granddaughter Allie: "One evening," said Allie, "when I was visiting Grandpa Snow in his room in the Salt Lake Temple, I remained until the doorkeepers had gone and the night watchman had not yet come in, so grandpa said he would take me to the main front entrance and let me out that way. He got his bunch of keys from the dresser. After we left his room and while we were still in the large corridor leading to the celestial room, I was walking several steps ahead of Grandpa when he stopped me saying: Wait a moment, Allie, I want to tell you something.

"It was right here that the Lord, Jesus Christ appeared to me. He stood about three feet above the floor. It looked like he stood on a plate of solid gold. Grandpa told me what a glorious personage the Savior is and described His hands, feet, countenance and beautiful white robes, all of which were of such glory of whiteness and brightness that he could hardly gaze upon Him. Then Grandpa came another step nearer me and put his right hand on my head and said: Now Granddaughter I want you to remember that this is the testimony of your Grandfather that he told you with his own lips that he actually saw the Savior here in the temple and talked with him face to face. Then we went on and Grandpa let me out of the main front door of the temple." (SMH, 11-14 1994 edition)

Melvin J. Ballard's Testimony: "I had sought the Lord...and that night I received a wonderful manifestation and an impression which has never left me. I was carried to this place, the Temple, into this room. I saw myself here with my brethren, and I was happy.... I was told there was one other privilege that was mine; and I was led into a room where I was informed I was to meet someone. As I entered the room, I saw, seated on a raised platform, the most glorious Being I have ever conceived of, and was taken forward to be introduced to him. As I approached He smiled, called my name, and stretched out His hands towards me. If I live to be a million years old, I shall never forget that smile. He put his arms around me and kissed me, as He took me into His bosom, and He blessed me until my whole being was thrilled. As He finished, I fell at His feet, and there saw the marks of the nails; and as I kissed them, with deep joy swelling through my whole being, I felt that I was in heaven indeed." (*Improvement Era*, October, 1932, Vol. 35, pp.714-715. As quoted in SMH, pp. 17-18, 1994 edition)

Jesus Christ, the Only Begotten Son of God was and is the literal son of God in the flesh as well as the elder Brother of all mankind in the spirit.

In Summary...

He is the Savior and Redeemer of all mankind.
He is the Messiah, the Anointed One.
He is the great "I Am" of the Old Testament.
He is the God of Abraham, Isaac, and Jacob.
He is the Mediator of the covenant between God and man.
He is the only one through and by whom men may come to the Father.

He descended below all things that he might rise above all things.

He is Alpha and Omega, the beginning and the end.

He is the resurrection and the life of all men.

He is the Holy One of Israel.

He is the God of the Jews, of the Nephites, the Lamanites, and all Israel.

He is the Lamb of God.

He is the light and life of the world.

He is in the express image of God the Eternal Father.

He is the King of all Israel.

He is the Father of all who abide his gospel.

He knew all things from the beginning and has made ample provisions for both the living and the dead.

He is the only one through whom salvation shall come. "There is none other name given under heaven save it be Jesus Christ...whereby man can be saved." (2 Nephi 25:20)

No other person has done so much for all the inhabitants of this earth. No name under heaven holds the hope for the world and its inhabitants. No other plan, philosophy, or way of life can bring salvation to man than the plan the Savior provided.

Jesus Christ is the God of this world, the Jehovah of the Old Testament, and the Lord and Savior of the New Testament. He is the one chosen of the Father to be our Savior and Redeemer, the one we sustained in the councils of heaven, he is the Only Begotten Son of God in the flesh and his is the only name under heaven whereby we must be saved.

CHAPTER FOUR
CHRIST'S GLORIOUS SECOND COMING

The second coming of Christ shall be as real as His first coming. His second coming shall be different in that it shall be witnessed by all the inhabitants of the earth, for His second coming shall be "as the light of the morning cometh out of the east, and shineth even unto the west, and covereth the whole earth." (IV, Matthew 24:27)

"As to the Second Coming, the time is fixed, the hour is set," said Elder Bruce R. McConkie, "and, speaking after the manner of the Lord, the day is soon to be. The appointed day can be neither advanced nor delayed. It will come at the decreed moment, chosen before the foundation of the earth was laid, and it can be neither hastened by righteousness nor put off by wickedness. It will be with our Lord's return as it was with his birth to Mary: the time of each coming was fixed by the Father." (NWAF, 591)

President Joseph Fielding Smith explained that Elder Orson F. Whitney used to write about living in the Saturday Evening of Time. President Smith continued, "This is the 6th day now drawing to its close.

When the Lord says it is today until his coming, that, I think, is what he has in mind, for he shall come in the morning of the Sabbath, or seventh day of the earth's temporal existence, to inaugurate the millennial reign and to take his rightful place as King of kings and Lord of lords, to rule and reign upon the earth, as it is his right." (DS 3:1)

President Joseph Fielding Smith said: "I was asked, not long ago, if I could tell when the Lord would come. I answered, Yes; and I answer, Yes, now. I know when he will come. He will come tomorrow. We have his word for it. Let me read it: 'Behold, now it is called today until the coming of the Son of Man, and verily it is a day of sacrifice, and a day for the tithing of my people; for he that is tithed shall not be burned at his coming. For after today cometh the burning—this is speaking after the manner of the Lord—for verily I say, tomorrow all the proud and they that do wickedly shall be as stubble; and I will burn them up, for I am the Lord of Hosts; and I will not spare any that remain in Babylon.' So the Lord is coming, I say, tomorrow." (DS 3:1)

The prophet Joseph Smith was anxious to know the time of the second coming of the Savior. And so he asked the Lord concerning his coming; and while asking the Lord, gave a sign and said, "In the days of Noah I set a bow in the heavens as a sign and token that in any year that the bow should be seen the Lord would not come; but there should be seed time and harvest during that year: but whenever you see the bow withdrawn, it shall be a token that there shall be famine, pestilence, and great distress among the nations, and that the coming of the Messiah is not far distant." (DPJS, 230)

Jesus' apostles asked the same questions. As Jesus sat upon the Mount of Olives, the disciples came unto him privately, saying, "...Tell us, when shall these things be which thou hast said concerning the destruction of the temple, and the Jews; And what is the sign of thy coming; and of the end of the world? (or the destruction of the wicked, which is the end of the world)." (IV, Matthew 24:4)

The Savior made known to them many of the signs of His coming: Many shall come in my name and deceive many. You shall be hated and afflicted and they shall kill you. Many false prophets shall arise and shall deceive many. Iniquity shall abound and the love of many shall wax cold. The abomination of desolation spoken of by Daniel concerning the destruction of Jerusalem shall come. False Christs and false prophets shall arise and shall show great signs and wonders. You shall hear of wars and rumors of wars. They shall say unto you, behold he is in the desert: And behold he is in the secret chambers. Nation shall rise against nation, and kingdom shall rise against kingdom. There shall be famines, pestilences, and earthquakes in divers places. And as it was in the days of Noah, so it shall be also at the coming of the Son of Man. And again, this gospel of the kingdom shall be preached in all the world, for a witness to all nations, and then shall the end come, or the destruction of the wicked. (see IV, Matthew 24:1-56, IV, Mark 13:1-61, IV, Luke 21:7-36)

The apostles were left thus to ponder and reflect upon the signs of the second coming of Christ, as given to them by the Savior.

There are many things that must be done before the

coming of the Savior in the clouds of Heaven. The Prophet Joseph Smith presented some items with regards to the Jews and Jerusalem.

"Judah must return, Jerusalem must be rebuilt, and the temple, and water come out from under the temple, and the waters of the Dead Sea be healed. It will take some time to rebuild the walls of the city and the temple, etc.; and all this must be done before the Son of Man will make his appearance." (DPJS, 236-237)

The healing of the Dead Sea and how it will be done has always been of interest to the Saints of the Church of Jesus Christ of Latter-day Saints. Standing on top of Masada, one can see that the lower part of the Dead Sea has fresh water in it. However, the majority of the Dead Sea is still a salt sea which can be learned from first-hand experience. Next to the shore of the dead sea are springs of fresh water where one may relieve oneself of the clinging salt.

Ezekiel explained how the Dead Sea would be healed. He said water would come from under the threshold of the temple. At first the waters were only to the ankles.

The water continued to come forth until a river was formed that could not be crossed over.

Many trees were observed on each side of the river, and finally, the water of the dead sea was healed.

Everywhere the river went it brought forth life, and there were exceeding many fish in the waters.

Trees were found on the river banks. Some trees were for food and others were for medicine. (see Ezekiel 47:1-12)

Perhaps the healing of the Dead Sea, with it's attendant blessings of trees both for food and for medicine: the exceeding many fish, and other living things the waters caused to be, may be of assistance to the Jewish people in their return to their homeland.

To return to the prophet's statement regarding the Jews and Jerusalem. "Judah must return, Jerusalem must be rebuilt, and the temple. And water come out from under the temple, and the waters of the Dead Sea be healed. It will take some time to rebuild the walls of the city and the temple, etc., and all this must be done before the Son of Man will make His appearance said the prophet." (DPJS, 236-237)

Since 1948, the Jews have been returning to the Holy Land. Long before that date, however, the prophet Joseph Smith called on Orson Hyde, a member of the council of the twelve apostles and a Jew to go and dedicate the land of Palestine for the return of the Jews. On the 24th day of October, 1841, standing on the Mount of Olives, overlooking Jerusalem, Orson Hyde offered his prayer.

"Grant, therefore, O Lord, in the name of Thy well-beloved Son, Jesus Christ, to remove the barrenness and sterility of this land, and let springs of living water break forth to water its thirsty soil. Let the vine and olive produce in their strength, and the fig tree bloom and flourish. Let the land become abundantly fruitful when possessed by its rightful heirs; let it again flow with plenty to feed the returning prodigals who come home with a spirit of grace and supplication; upon it let the clouds distil virtue and richness, and let the fields smile with plenty. Let the flocks and herds greatly increase and multiply upon the mountains and the hills; and let Thy great kindness conquer and subdue the unbelief of Thy people. Do Thou take from them their stony heart, and give them a heart fresh; and may the Sun of Thy favor dispel the cold mists of darkness which have beclouded their atmosphere. Incline them [the Jews] to gather in upon this land according to Thy word. Let them come like clouds and like doves to their windows. Let the large ships of the nations bring them from the distant isles; and let kings become their nursing fathers, and queens with motherly fondness wipe the tear of sorrow from their eye." (HC 4:457)

Brigham Young said regarding the Jewish people: "We have a great desire for their [Jews] welfare, and are looking for the time soon to come when they will gather to Jerusalem, build up the city and the land of Palestine, and prepare for the coming of the Messiah." (JD 11:279)

But Joseph Fielding Smith said: "Not many of the Jews...will believe in Christ before he comes. The Book of Mormon tells us that they shall begin to believe in him. They are now beginning to believe in him. The Jews today look upon Christ as a great Rabbi. They have accepted him as one of their great teachers; they have said that, 'He is Jew of Jew, the greatest

Rabbi of them all,' as one has stated it." President Smith points out "When the gospel was restored in 1830, if a Jew had mentioned the name of Christ in one of the synagogues, he would have been rebuked. Had a rabbi referred to him, the congregation would have arisen and left the building. And so, we see the sentiment has changed.... They are beginning to believe in Christ, and some of them are accepting the gospel.

"But in the main they will gather to Jerusalem in their unbelief; the gospel will be preached to them; some of them will believe. Not all of the Gentiles have believed when the gospel has been proclaimed to them, but the great body of the Jews who are assembled there will not receive Christ as their Redeemer until he comes himself and makes himself manifest unto them." (DS 3:9)

The rebuilding of Jerusalem, the temple, the city and the walls of the city, the healing of the Dead Sea are all yet to be accomplished. We learn from the Book of Mormon that the old city of Jerusalem will be rebuilt and become a Holy City unto the Lord and also that a New Jerusalem shall be built on the American continent.

"Behold, Ether saw the days of Christ, and he spake concerning a New Jerusalem upon this land. And he spake also concerning the house of Israel, and the Jerusalem from whence Lehi should come—after it should be destroyed it should be built up again, a holy city unto the Lord;... The remnant of the house of Joseph shall be built upon this land; and it shall be a land of their inheritance; and they shall build up a holy city unto the Lord, like unto the Jerusalem of old;... And there shall be a new heaven and a new earth; and they shall be like unto the old save the old have passed away and all things have become new. And then cometh the New Jerusalem; and blessed are they who dwell therein, for it is they whose garments are white through the blood of the Lamb; and they are they who are numbered among the remnant of the seed of Joseph, who were of the house of Israel. And then also cometh the Jerusalem of old; and the inhabitants thereof, blessed are they, for they have been washed in the blood of the Lamb; and they are they who were scattered and gathered in from the four quarters of the earth, and from the north countries, and are partakers of the fulfilling of the covenant which God made with their father, Abraham. (Ether 13:4-5, 8-11)

The Prophet Joseph Smith was instructed by the Lord to counsel the Saints to:

"Go ye out of Babylon; gather ye out from among the nations, from the four winds, from one end of heaven to the other. Send forth the elders of my church unto the nations which are afar off; unto the islands of the sea; send forth unto foreign lands; call upon all nations, first upon the Gentiles and then upon the Jews. And behold, and lo, this shall be their cry, and the voice of the Lord unto all people: Go ye forth unto the land of Zion, that the borders of my people may be enlarged, and that her stakes may be strengthened, and that Zion may go forth unto the regions round about.... And let them who be of Judah flee unto Jerusalem, unto the mountains of the Lord's house. Go ye out from among the nations, even from Babylon, from the midst of wickedness, which is spiritual Babylon." (D&C 133:7-9, 13-14)

There must be the gathering of Israel before Christ comes to earth. The Savior said to his apostles on the

Mount of Olives: "And now I show unto you a parable. Behold, wheresoever the carcass is, there will the eagles be gathered together; so likewise shall mine elect be gathered from the four quarters of the earth.... For the Son of Man shall come, and he shall send his angels before him with the great sound of a trumpet, and they shall gather together the remainder of his elect from the four winds; from one end of heaven to the other." (IV, Matthew 24:28, 40)

The work of gathering of Israel preparatory to the Second Coming of Christ was a topic of great interest to the Prophet Joseph Smith, who stated: "All that the prophets that have written, from the days of righteous Abel, down to the last man that has left any testimony on record for our consideration, in speaking of the salvation of Israel in the last days, goes directly to show that it consists in the work of the gathering." (DPJS, 190-191)

The tenth Article of Faith explains the belief of the Church concerning the gathering: "We believe in the literal gathering of Israel and in the restoration of the Ten Tribes; that Zion (the New Jerusalem) will be built upon the American continent; that Christ will reign personally upon the earth; and, that the earth will be renewed and receive its paradisiacal glory."

"What was the object of the gathering of the Jews, or the people of God in any age of the world?" asked the Prophet Joseph Smith, and then he answered: "The main object was to build unto the Lord a house whereby He could reveal unto His people the ordinances of His house and the glories of His kingdom, and teach the people the way of salvation; for there are certain ordinances and principles that, when they are taught and practiced, must be done in a place or house built for that purpose.

"It was the design of the councils of heaven before the world was, that the principles and laws of the priesthood should be predicated upon the gathering of the people in every age of the world. Jesus did everything to gather the people, and they would not be gathered, and He therefore poured out curses upon them. Ordinances instituted in the heavens before the foundation of the world, in the priesthood, for the salvation of men, are not to be altered or changed. All must be saved on the same principles.

"It is for the same purpose that God gathers together His people in the last days, to build unto the Lord a house to prepare them for the ordinances and endowments, washings and anointings, etc. One of the ordinances of the house of the Lord is baptism for the dead..." (DPJS, 190)

"...if we are not sanctified and gathered to the places God has appointed,... we must fall; we cannot stand; we cannot be saved; for God will gather out his Saints from the Gentiles, and then comes desolation and destruction, and none can escape except the pure in heart who are gathered." (DPJS, 193)

The prophet explained how Israel would be gathered: "Our missionaries are going forth to different nations, and in Germany, Palestine, New Holland, Australia, the East Indies, and other places, the Standard of Truth has been erected; no unhallowed hand can stop the work from progressing; persecutions may rage, mobs may combine, armies may assemble, calumny may defame, but the truth of God will go forth boldly, nobly, and independent, till it has penetrated every continent, visited every clime, swept every country, and sounded in every ear, till the purposes of God shall be accomplished, and the Great Jehovah shall say the work is done." (DPJS, 280)

He planned that missionaries would be called to go to their own people to carry the Standard of Truth. For instance, he said: "Take Jacob Zundell and Frederick H. Moeser, and send them to Germany; and when you meet with an Arab, send him to Arabia; when you find an Italian, send him to Italy; and a Frenchman, to France; or an Indian, that is suitable, send him among the Indians. Send them to the different places where they belong. Send somebody to Central America and to all Spanish America; and don't let a single corner of the earth go without a mission." (DPJS, 173)

The two places of gathering are Zion and Old Jerusalem. The Prophet said: "You know there has been great discussion in relation to Zion—where it is, and where the gathering of the dispensation is, and which I am now going to tell you. The prophets have spoken and written upon it; but I will make a proclamation that will cover a broader ground. *The whole of America is Zion itself from north to south, and is described by the prophets, who declare that it is the Zion where the mountain of the Lord should be, and that it should be in the center of the land."* (DPJS, 188)

"The city of Zion spoken of by David, in the one hundred and second Psalm, will be built upon the land of America, 'And the ransomed of the Lord shall return, and come to Zion with songs and everlasting joy upon their heads.' (Isaiah 35:10.) And then they will be delivered from the overflowing scourge that shall pass through the land. But Judah shall obtain deliverance at Jerusalem." (DPJS, 188)

President Joseph Fielding Smith said that Zion and Jerusalem are the two world capitals. "When Joseph Smith translated the *Book of Mormon*, he learned that America is the land of Zion which was given to Joseph and his children and that on this land the City Zion, or New Jerusalem, is to be built. He also learned that Jerusalem in Palestine is to be rebuilt and become a holy city. These two cities, one in the land of Zion and one in Palestine, are to become capitals for the kingdom of God during the millennium." (DS 3:71)

He quoted Isaiah who said: "And it shall come to pass in the last days, that the mountain of the Lord's house shall be established in the top of the mountains, and shall be exalted above the hills; and all nations shall flow unto it. And many people shall go and say, Come ye, and let us go up to the mountain of the Lord, to the house of the God of Jacob; and he will teach us of his ways, and we will walk in his paths: for out of Zion shall go forth the law, and the word of the Lord from Jerusalem." (IV, Isaiah 2:2)

Then he explained that "The statement is very clear that two separate cities, or centers, are mentioned by Isaiah. In modern revelation this is confirmed, and we are informed just where the city of Zion—which is the New Jerusalem—shall be built. In order to get a proper understanding of this question, it is necessary to explain the fact that Palestine is to be the gathering place of the tribe of Judah and 'the children of Israel his companions,' after their long dispersion as predicted by the prophets. America is the land of Zion. It was given to Joseph, son of Jacob, and his descendants to be an everlasting inheritance. The children of Ephraim (son of Joseph) and 'all the house of Israel his companions,' will be gathered to Zion, or America." (DS 3:67-68)

John the Beloved while on the Isle of Patmos said that the everlasting gospel was to be preached unto them that dwell on the earth, and to every nation and kindred, and tongue, and people. "Saying with a loud voice, Fear God, and give glory to Him; for the hour of His judgment is come: and worship him that made heaven, and earth, and the sea, and the fountains of waters." (IV, Revelation 14:7)

To the Prophet Joseph Smith the Lord said, "The voice of the Lord is unto all men and there is none to escape; And there is no eye that shall not see, neither ear that shall not hear, neither heart that shall not be penetrated...wherefore the voice of the Lord is unto the ends of the earth, that all that will hear may hear." (D&C 1:2, 11)

Thus we learn that the warning voice of the Lord has been given to every nation and kindred and tongue and people even unto all men to the ends of the earth.

President John Taylor explained that the Lord has always warned the wicked of the things that were to come. Said he: "Some people talk about the world being burned up, about plagues, pestilence, famine, sword, and ruin, and all these things being instantaneous. Now it would not be just for the Lord to punish the inhabitants of the earth without warning. For if the world are ignorant of god, they cannot altogether be blamed for it;...Before the Lord destroyed the inhabitants of the old world, he sent Enoch and Noah to warn them. Before the Lord destroyed Sodom and Gomorrah, he sent Lot into their midst. Before the Children of Israel were carried captive to Babylon, they were warned of it by the Prophets; and before Jerusalem was destroyed, the inhabitants had the testimony of our Lord, and his Disciples. And so will it be in the last days; and as it is the world that is concerned, the world will have to be warned." (GG, chapter 11)

Joseph Fielding Smith told of the calamities that would come from rejecting the gospel: "The distress and perplexity, bloodshed and terror, selfish ambition of despotic rulers, such as the world has never before seen, all indicate that the great and dreadful day of the Lord is very near, even at our doors. We have been warned by the prophets from the beginning of time. They have declared, by revelation from the Lord, that in this present day, confusion, bloodshed, misery, plague, famine, earthquake, and other calamities, would cover the face of the earth. The Lord told his disciples of these dreadful scenes and said men's hearts would fail them because of these things coming upon the earth...." (DS 3:19)

Rejection of the Gospel causes destruction on the earth. In an article written in the Millennial Star, Elder Charles W. Penrose stated: "Through the rejection of this Gospel, which 'Shall be preached to all the world as a witness' of the coming of Christ, the world will increase in confusion, doubt, and horrible strife. As the upright in heart, the meek of the earth, withdraw from their midst, so will the spirit of God also be withdrawn from them. The darkness upon their minds in relation to eternal things will become blacker, nations will engage in frightful and bloody warfare, the crimes which are now becoming so frequent will be of continual occurrence, the ties that bind together families and kindred will be disregarded and violated, the passions of human nature will be put to the vilest uses, the very elements around will seem to be affected by the national and social convulsions that will agitate the world, and storms, earthquakes, and appalling disasters by sea and land will cause terror and dismay among the people; new diseases will silently eat their ghastly way through the ranks of the wicked; the earth, soaked with gore and defiled with the filthiness of her inhabitants, will begin to withhold her fruits in their season; the waves of the sea will heave themselves beyond their bounds, and all things will be in commotion; and in the midst of all these calamities, the masterminds among nations will be taken away, and fear will take hold of the hearts of all men." (MS 21:582)

Wilford Woodruff said: "My testimony is this unto all men and nations, that you live in the day and the hour of the judgments of God Almighty. You live in the day and generation when the God of Israel has set his hand to perform his work, his strange work in the latter days. You live in the age in which God will bring to pass the fulfillment of that word of prophecy and prediction which has been spoken by all the prophets since the world began, and the fulfillment of these revelations will involve the destiny of the whole world, Jew and Gentile, rich and poor, high and low, saint and sinner, Babylon and Zion." (MS 41:241ff)

Joseph Fielding Smith explained that: "Apostate Christianity carries no warning of second coming. It is well understood that the teachings of the so-called Christian churches have been declared in all the world for many hundreds of years. In all lands churches have been organized and ministers have proclaimed their teachings. There is nothing peculiar about their message in relation to the present age—nothing distinctive which would mark any one or all of them as having the special declaration of the gospel of the kingdom which was promised as a witness in the latter days.

"The implication in these words of our Lord—that 'this gospel of the kingdom shall be preached in all the world for a witness unto all nations; and then shall the end come'—the implication is that in the last days the Lord would give as a sign to all nations the sending anew of the message of the gospel of the kingdom and that it would be different from the teachings then being taught and received among the nations. Otherwise how could it be distinguished and accepted as a sign of his second coming?" (DS 3:5)

And as the Savior said to His apostles on the Mount of Olives: "And again, this gospel of the kingdom shall be preached in all the world, for a witness unto all nations, and then shall the end come, or the destruction of the wicked;" (IV, Matthew 24:32)

Joseph Smith declared: "The servants of God will not have gone over the nations of the Gentiles, with a warning voice, until the destroying angel will commence to waste the inhabitants of the earth, and there will be wars and rumors of wars, signs in the heavens above and on the earth beneath, the sun turned into darkness and the moon to blood, earthquakes in divers places, the seas heaving beyond their bounds; then will appear one grand sign of the Son of Man in heaven. But what will the world do? They will say it is a planet, a comet, etc. But the Son of Man will come as the sign of the coming of the Son of Man, which will be as the light of the morning cometh out of the east." (DPJS, 237)

The Savior likewise testified of the brightness of His coming when he said to His apostles on the Mount of Olives: "For as the light of the morning cometh out of the east, and shineth even unto the west, and cov-ereth the whole earth; so shall also the coming of the Son of Man be." (IV, Matthew 24:27)

The Savior has made and will also make other appearances before His glorious coming. He came to Joseph Smith and Sidney Rigdon as recorded in the vision of the glories, section 76 of the Doctrine and Covenants—speaking of the Only Begotten Son of God "Of whom we bear record; and the record which we bear is the fullness of the gospel of Jesus Christ, who is the Son, whom we saw and with whom we conversed in the Heavenly vision." (D&C 76:14)

In the Kirtland Temple the Prophet Joseph Smith and Oliver Cowdery recorded "We saw the Lord stand-ing upon the breastwork of the pulpit, before us; and under his feet was a paved work of pure gold, in color like amber. His eyes were as a flame of fire; the hair of his head was white like the pure snow; His counte-nance shown above the brightness of the sun; and his voice was as the sound of the rushing of great waters, even the voice of Jehovah saying: I am the first and the last; I am he who liveth, I am he who was slain; I am your advocate with the Father." (D&C 110:2-4)

There will be another great event in which the Savior will appear unbeknown to the world. This will be in the valley of Adam-ondi-Ahman, an occasion somewhat like this occurred three years previous to the death of Adam.

President Joseph Fielding Smith referred to this account as recorded in D&C 107: "Three years before the death of Adam, he called together his children, including all the faithful down to the generation of Methuselah, 'with the residue of his posterity who were righteous, into the valley of Adam-ondi-Ahman, and there bestowed upon them his last blessing.' (D&C 107:53) At this grand gathering the Lord appeared and administered comfort unto Adam, and said unto him: 'I have set thee to be at the head; a multitude of nations shall come of thee, and thou art a prince over them forever.' The assembly arose and blessed Adam, and called him Michael, the prince, the arch-angel. Then Adam stood up in the midst of the congregation—and no such a gathering on any other occasion has this world ever seen—and notwithstanding he was bowed down with age, being full of the Holy ghost, (he) predicted whatsoever should befall his posterity unto the last generation. "All of this is written in the Book of Enoch which shall be revealed in due time." (D&C 107:54-57)

President Joseph Fielding Smith described what would take place in the Valley of Adam-ondi-Ahman: "Not many years hence there shall be another gathering of high priests and righteous souls in the same valley of Adam-ondi-Ahman. At this gathering, Adam, the Ancient of Days, will again be present. At this time the vision which Daniel saw will be enacted. The Ancient of Days will sit. There will stand before him those who have held the keys of all dispensations, who shall render up their stewardships to the first Patriarch of the race, who holds the keys of salvation. This shall be a day of judgement and preparation....

"It was in the night vision that all this was shown to Daniel, and he saw the Son of Man come to the grand council, as he did to the first grand council in the alley of Adam-ondi-Ahman, and there he received the keys from Adam....

"This council in the valley of Adam-ondi-Ahman is

to be of the greatest importance to this world. At that time there will be a transfer of authority from the usurper and impostor, Lucifer, to the rightful King, Jesus Christ. Judgement will be set and all who have held keys will make their reports and deliver their stewardships, as they shall be required. Adam will direct this judgment, and then he will make his report, as the one holding the keys for this earth, to his Superior Officer, Jesus Christ. Our Lord will then assume the reins of government; directions will be given to the Priesthood there assembled. This grand council of priesthood will be composed, not only of those who are faithful who now dwell on this earth, but also of the prophets and apostles of old, who have had directing authority. Others may also be there, but if so they will be there by appointment, for this is to be an official council called to attend to the most momentous matters concerning the destiny of this earth.

"When this gathering is held, the world will not know of it; the members of the Church at large will not know of it, yet it shall be preparatory to the coming in the clouds of glory of our Savior Jesus Christ as the

Prophet Joseph Smith has said. The world cannot know of it. The Saints cannot know of it—except those who officially shall be called into this council—for it shall proceed the coming of the Jesus Christ as a thief in the night, unbeknown to all the world." (WP 288-291)

The great and dreadful events of the Second Coming will be of a dual nature. It will be a great day for the righteous, but it will be a dreadful day for the wicked. President Charles W. Penrose, in his article, "The Second Advent" declared,

"The tongue of man falters and the pen drops from the hand of the writer, as the mind is rapt in contemplation of the sublime and awful majesty of his coming to take vengeance on the ungodly and to reign as King of the whole earth.

"He comes! The earth shakes, and the tall mountains tremble, the mighty deep rolls back to the north as in fear, and the rent skies glow like molten brass. He comes! The dead saints burst forth from their tombs, and "those who are alive and remain" are "caught up" with them to meet him. The ungodly rush to hide themselves from his presence, and call upon the quivering rocks to cover them. He comes with all the hosts of the righteous glorified. The breath of his lips strikes death to the wicked. His glory is a consuming fire. The proud and rebellious are as stubble; they are burned and "left neither root nor branch." He sweeps the earth "as with the besom broom of destruction." He deluges the earth with the fiery floods of his wrath, and the filthiness and abominations of the world are consumed. Satan and his dark hosts are taken and bound—the prince of the power of the air has lost his dominion, for He whose right is to reign has come, and "the kingdoms of this world have become the kingdoms of our Lord and of his Christ." (MS, Sept. 1859)

Brigham Young asked the question: "Are you prepared for the day of vengeance to come, when the Lord will consume the wicked by the brightness of his coming?... Let our anxiety be centered upon this one thing, the sanctification of our hearts, the purifying of our own affections, the preparing of ourselves for the approach of the events that are hastening upon us.... This should be our daily prayer, and not to be in a hurry to see the overthrow of the wicked....

Seek to have the Spirit of Christ, that we may wait patiently the time of the Lord, and prepare ourselves for the times that are coming. This is our duty." (JD 9:3)

The actual events of the second coming were revealed to the Prophet Joseph Smith in that great revelation known as the appendix to the Doctrine and Covenants (Section 133) verse 19 is the Lord's invitation to prepare for His coming and to go forth to meet him: "Wherefore, prepare ye for the coming of the Bridegroom: Go ye, go ye out to meet Him."

He will be everywhere present, as said in verse 20: "For behold, he shall stand upon the mount of Olivet, and upon the mighty ocean, even the great deep, and upon the islands of the sea, and upon the land of Zion."

Verse 21: His voice is heard among all people: "And he shall utter his voice out of Zion, and he shall speak from Jerusalem, and his voice shall be heard among all people;"

Verses 22-25: He speaks of the great changes to take place, (The earth was divided in the days of peleg—He spake of it's return to it's former creation):

"And it shall be a voice as the voice of many waters, and as the voice of a great thunder, which shall break down the mountains, and the valleys shall not be found. He shall command the great deep, and it shall be driven back into the north countries, and the islands shall become one land; And the land of Jerusalem and the land of Zion shall be turned back into their own place, and the earth shall be like as it was in the days before it was divided. And the Lord, even the Savior, shall stand in the midst of his people, and shall reign over all flesh."

Verses 26-29: Prophets and people from the North and how they will be assisted in making their journey: "And they who are in the north countries shall come in remembrance before the Lord; and their prophets shall hear his voice, and shall no longer stay themselves; and they shall smite the rocks, and the ice shall flow down at their presence. And an highway shall be cast up in the midst of the great deep. Their enemies shall become a prey unto them. And in the barren deserts there shall come forth pools of living water; and the parched ground shall no longer be a thirsty land."

Verses 30-35: Those from the north countries shall bring rich treasures to Ephraim and they shall be crowned with glory by the servants of Ephraim. Judah shall also be sanctified: "And they shall bring forth their rich treasures unto the children of Ephraim, my servants. And the boundaries of the everlasting hills shall tremble at their presence. And there shall they fall down and be crowned with glory, even in Zion, by the hands of the servants of the Lord, even the children of Ephraim. And they shall be filled with songs of ever-lasting joy. Behold, this is the blessing of the everlast-ing God upon the tribes of Israel, and the richer bless-ing upon the head of Ephraim and his fellows. And they also of the tribe of Judah, after their pain shall be sanctified in holiness before the Lord, to dwell in his presence day and night, forever and ever."

In section 45 of the Doctrine and Covenants, it was made known that the Jews shall look upon the Savior and shall say: "What are these wounds in thine hands and in thy feet? Then shall they know that I am the Lord; for I will say with them: these wounds are the wounds with which I was wounded in the house of my friends. I am he who was lifted up. I am Jesus that was crucified. I am the Son of God.

And then shall they weep because of their iniquities; then shall they lament because they persecuted their King." (D&C 45:51-53).

Continuing in D&C 133:45: Great blessings are in store for those who have waited for the Lord: "For since the beginning of the world have not men heard nor perceived by the ear, neither hath any eye seen, O God, besides thee, how great things thou hast prepared for him that waiteth for thee."

Verses 46-48: Savior to come in dyed garments in glorious apparel and traveling in greatness of his strength: "And it shall be said: Who is this that cometh down from God in heaven with dyed garments; yea, from the regions which are not known, clothed in his glorious apparel, traveling in the greatness of his strength? And he shall say: I am he who spake in righteousness, mighty to save. And the Lord shall be red in his apparel, and his garments like him that treadeth in the wine-vat."

Verse 49: His glory shall hide the sun: "And so

great shall be the glory of his presence that the sun shall hide his face in shame, and the moon shall withhold its light, and the stars shall be hurled from their places."

Verse 56: The saints shall come forth on the right hand of God both on Mount Zion and the City of New Jerusalem: "And the graves of the saints shall be opened; and they shall come forth and stand on the right hand of the Lamb, when he shall stand upon Mount Zion, and upon the holy city, the New Jerusalem; and they shall sing the song of the Lamb, day and night forever and ever." (D&C 133:19-56)

The revelations have declared that "all things shall be in commotion" when Christ comes so much so that "men's hearts shall fail them; for fear shall come upon all people." (D&C 88:91) And at the coming of the Lord, "angels shall fly through the midst of heaven, crying with a loud voice, sounding the trump of God, saying: Prepare ye, prepare ye, O inhabitants of the earth; for the judgment of our God is come. Behold, and lo, the Bridegroom cometh; go ye out to meet him. And immediately there shall appear a great sign in heaven, and all people shall see it together." (D&C 88:92-93)

Then shall the tares of the earth be bound into bundles and be made ready to be burned.

"And there shall be silence in heaven for the space of half an hour; and immediately after shall the curtain of heaven be unfolded, as a scroll is unfolded after it is rolled up, and the face of the Lord shall be unveiled;" (D&C 88:95)

Elder Orson Pratt said: "Whether the half hour here spoken of is according to our reckoning—thirty minutes, or whether it be according to the reckoning of the Lord we do not know. We know that the word hour is used in some portions of the Scriptures to represent quite a lengthy period of time. For instance, we, the Latter-day Saints, are living in the eleventh hour, that is the eleventh period of time; and for aught we know the half hour during which silence is to prevail in heaven may be quite an extensive period of time. During the period of silence all things are perfectly still; no angels flying during the half hour; no trumpets sounding; no noise in the heavens above; but immediately after this great silence the curtain of heaven shall be unfolded as a scroll is unfolded." (JD 16:328)

Then is revealed the great events regarding the coming forth of all the inhabitants of the earth.

"...And the saints that are upon the earth, who are alive, shall be quickened and be caught up to meet him.

"And they who have slept in their graves shall come forth, for their graves shall be opened; and they also shall be caught up to meet him in the midst of the pillar of heaven—

"They are Christ's, the first fruits, they who shall descend with him first, and they who are on the earth and in their graves, who are first caught up to meet him; and all this by the voice of the sounding of the trump of the angel of God.

"And after this another angel shall sound, which is the second trump; and then cometh the redemption of those who are Christ's at his coming; who have received their part in that prison which is prepared for them, that they might receive the gospel, and be judged according to men in the flesh.

"And again, another trump shall sound, which is the

third trump; and then come the spirits of men who are to be judged, and are found under condemnation;

"And these are the rest of the dead; and they live not again until the thousand years are ended, neither again, until the end of the earth.

"And another trump shall sound, which is the fourth trump, saying: There are found among those who are to remain until that great and last day, even the end, who shall remain filthy still." (D&C 88:96-102)

Wilford Woodruff was shown the times of resurrection by an heavenly messenger. President Woodruff said: "While I was upon my knees praying, my room was filled with light. I looked and a messenger stood by my side. I arose, and this personage told me he had come to instruct me. He presented before me a panorama. He told me he wanted me to see with my eyes and understand with my mind what was coming to pass in the earth before the coming of the Son of Man. He commenced with what the revelations say about the sun being turned to darkness, the moon to blood, and the stars falling from heaven. Those things were all presented to me one after another, as they will be, I suppose, when they are manifest before the coming of the Son of Man. Then he showed me the resurrection of the dead—what is termed the first and second resurrection. In the first resurrection I saw no graves nor anyone raised from the grave. I saw legions of celestial beings, men and women who had received the gospel all clothed in white robes. In the form they were presented to me, they had already been raised from the grave. After this he showed me what is termed the second resurrection. Vast fields of graves were before me, and the Spirit of God rested upon the earth like a shower of gentle rain, and when that fell upon the graves they were opened, and an immense host of human beings came forth. They were just as diversified in their dress as we are here, or as they were laid down. This personage taught me with regard to these things." (Wilford Woodruff, MS 76:612)

Orson Pratt said of those who would accompany the Savior at His coming:

"Who will be with Jesus when he appears? The decree has gone forth, saying, Mine Apostles who were with me in Jerusalem shall be clothed in glory and be with me. The brightness of their countenance will shine forth with all that refulgence and fullness of splendor that shall surround the Son of Man when he appears.... There will be all the former-day Saints, Enoch and his city, with all the greatness and splendor that surround them; there will be Abraham, Isaac, and Jacob, as they sit upon their thrones, together with all the persons that have been redeemed and brought near unto the presence of God. All will be unfolded and unveiled, and all this will be for the wicked to look upon, as well as the righteous; for the wicked will not as yet have been destroyed. When this takes place, there will be Latter-day saints living upon the earth, and they will ascend and mingle themselves with that vast throng; for they will be filled with anxiety to go where the Saints of the Church of the Firstborn are, and the Church of the Firstborn will feel an anxiety to come and meet with the Saints on earth, and this will bring the general assembly of the redeemed into one;" (JD 8:51)

The Prophet Joseph Smith said "When the Savior shall appear we shall see him as he is. We shall see that he is a man like ourselves, and that same sociality which exists among us here will exists among us there, only it will be coupled with eternal glory, which glory we do not now enjoy." (D&C 130:1-2)

President Charles W. Penrose said: "...when He comes we expect it will be Himself—Jesus of Nazareth, our Elder Brother, the first-born of God in the spirit world, the Only Begotten of God in flesh. We expect that He will come and reign over the earth as King of kings and Lord of lords...." (JD 25:222)

Enoch, his people, and their city were caught up into heaven and have walked and talked with God. The Lord called the people of Enoch, Zion, because they were of one heart and one mind and dwelt in righteousness.

"And the Lord said unto Enoch: As I live, even so will I come in the last days, in the days of wickedness and vengeance, to fulfil the oath which I have made unto you concerning the children of Noah;

"And the day shall come that the earth shall rest, but before that day the heavens shall be darkened, and a veil of darkness shall cover the earth; and the heavens shall shake, and also the earth; and great tribulations shall be among the children of men, but my people will I preserve;

"And righteousness will I send down out of heaven; and truth will I send forth out of the earth, to bear testimony of mine Only Begotten; his resurrection from the dead; yea, and also the resurrection of all men; and righteousness and truth will I cause to sweep the earth as with a flood, to gather out mine elect from the four quarters of the earth, unto a place which I shall prepare, an Holy City, that my people may gird up their loins, and be looking forth for the time of my coming; for there shall be my tabernacle, and it shall be called Zion, a New Jerusalem.

"And the Lord said unto Enoch: Then shalt thou and all thy city meet them there, and we will receive them into our bosom, and they shall see us; and we will fall upon their necks, and they shall fall upon our necks, and we will kiss each other;

"And there shall be mine abode, and it shall be Zion, which shall come forth out of all the creations which I have made; and for the space of a thousand years the earth shall rest." (Moses 7:60-64)